LOVE ON THE STREETS

D1432760

Pitt Poetry Series
Ed Ochester, Editor

Love on the Streets

SELECTED AND NEW POEMS

Sharon Doubiago

University of
Pittsburgh Press

Published by the University of Pittsburgh Press, Pittsburgh, Pa., 15260
Copyright © 2008, Sharon Doubiago
All rights reserved
Manufactured in the United States of America
Printed on acid-free paper
10 9 8 7 6 5 4 3 2 1
ISBN 13: 978-0-8229-6008-9
ISBN 10: 0-8229-6008-7

For Ryan Axel Darien Menez Bishara Doubiago

For the poets

It is the need to enter what we loosely call the vision to be one with the Imago Mundi, that image of the world we each carry within us as possibility itself.

—ROBERT CREELEY

The telling of our journeys is as much religion as the ceremonies themselves.

—THE HOPI

We, one generation through thousands of lifetimes: women and men, who are more and more filled with the child we will bear.

—RAINER MARIA RILKE

But gods always face two-ways
So let us search the old highways.

—H. D.

Ay, many flowering islands lie
In the waters of wide Agony. . . .

—PERCY BYSSHE SHELLEY

Yo hatch katchkani
Manan yo hatch katchkani
Chaimita tapukui

CONTENTS

NEW POEMS (2000–2008)

from

HARD COUNTRY

1982

To create a new desire: To remember the dis-
membered

—MERIDEL LE SUEUR

Your face is strange
And the smell of your garments
But your soul is familiar
As if in dreams our thoughts
had visited one another

Often from unremembering sleep
I wake delicately glowing
Now I know what my heart was doing

Now I know why when we met
It slipped
So easily into loving

—"WASHOE-PAIUTE GLYPH"
  (translated by Mary Austin, 1904)

Signal Hill √

My father leaves us in the car
and drinks beer in the Hilltop Bar.
The red neon woman who wears only
a ruffled apron and high heels
carries a tray of drinks
around and around the top of the hill
to the giant robots that pump
the fields.

In her red light my baby
brother and sister in the backseat of the car
are contorted in screams Daddy doesn't hear
over the jukebox and high squeals
of the barmaid I never see and wonder
if she too wears no clothes.
I hear her cry *ah Babes!*
We come here every Friday when he gets paid
but my brother and sister are still afraid
of the creatures nodding in the dark
we are parked between.

The city spreads beneath us
in a rainbow-spilled oil puddle.
The harbor is lit with battleships
that strain at their ropes
toward bigger war across the sea.

The dirty men keep driving up beside us.
I sit in the mother's seat
and they say to me the things men say
to mothers.

I study her nipples that seem so gay
and wonder if mine will get that way.
Far below on the shore of the Pike

a man sits on top of the neon needle
for months just to break a record.
One man says of him as he runs
his middle finger across the dewy window
of my face,
Tough, not gettin' any.

When Daddy comes through the door
beneath the spinning neon lady
it is the only time I ever see him
happy. Now we drive the cold side
of Signal Hill, the backside of the city and sea
so dark even in the middle of the twentieth century
they hide the dying, the ones
they still can't cure, my mother
in her sanitarium.

We drive across the starry oil field
to her window where she lies
in the contagion ward we kids cannot go near.
My father taps on her dark window
and soon my mother lifts the pane
and puts her porcelain hand
out into the dark for him.

He puts one of his
on one of her large breasts
that are not like the red neon woman's
and sometimes lays his head
on her white arm that knows no sun
and between the groans of the field
letting go its oil
I hear him sigh
oh, honey, and sometimes
jesus

I Was Born Coming to the Sea

I was born in Seaside Hospital on a Long Beach.
The buoy I heard calling from the sea
was a boy calling me
a year to the day they left Ducktown, Tennessee.
While I was coming, Daddy rode the rails
to catch the wheat harvest in Washington,
Mama waitressed the last road west,
a Japanese café at the end of Redondo Beach pier.
We rode the Midnight Ghost, Daddy and I gone north for some money,
while Mama and I at the sunset end of the world
brought food from across the sea.

Mama walked all day the hilly streets
above the long sea the day I was born,
the new city risen from the earthquake of '38.
The buoy I heard calling was a sailor who cried
from Japanese war, *don't bring a child
into this world*, everyone told them.
But they laughed. Mama was an orphan.
I felt her hold me as her mother had held her
through the orphanage walls. All my life
I've heard them laughing in the dark,
the sea lapping at the doors,
the gulls flapping in the windows,
the boy calling through the storm.

Thanksgivings we were too poor for turkey.
I pointed to a seagull, said my first sentence.
That's okay, Mama, Daddy can shoot an ea-gull.
When the ships came in from war, Friday nights,
payday when there was work, we went down to the Pike,
ate shrimp from Shrimpy Joe's, so cheap we bought bagfuls.
We watched the boys come home to neon,
to toothless, grinning, red-lipped women who tattooed
Mother on their chests.

Then we drove out the shaky night docks of Terminal Island,
sat on the foggy edge beneath groaning oil wells
and the dark squeaky hulls of returned battleships.
They told me the sound was a boy out there
telling boats how to come in through the fog.
I listened to the waves slapping him around.
I heard his crying, his lonely orphanage in the sea.
When we fished, I cast my line to him, I was coming
to the sea when I was born,
the buoy I heard through water and storm
was a boy calling me.

Father

I am like you, Mama always said.
Often we went fishing.
It takes patience and silence
to be a fisherman.
Most fail, you always said.

I am like you, Mama always said,
and if I reach back far enough
we are fishing again from the narrow rock ledge
that jettied the ocean at Seal Beach.
We crawled out to where crabs and unnameables crawled
out of dark seaweedy crevices, the dark holes
the ocean kept screaming up from.
We sat there, always on the dark side, for hours.
days.

It takes patience and silence
to be a fisherman.
We sat in the cold, cruel spray
of wave after wave churning to shore,
and with the contorted fishy bodies
of fishermen, old, toothless, bearded,
their awful cries above the cries of gulls
after deserted mussel.
bait.

I am like you, Daddy, Mama always said.
Your body a great melancholy night in which I sat
beneath your heart
in terrible silence
and fished.

The old men danced as the day
moved on, those
fishers, those broken
bearded kings, those

Ahabs.
As the flaming ball fell
to the water line between my thighs
I was a drowned creature
drifting hundreds of years
in the unspeakable
foundations.

Unwarped, unarguable shapes
glided to and fro
before my passive eyes.
Did I ever catch a fish?
Did I ever want to?
I wanted only
to sit there longer
on the dry landside of my father
knowing the shadow of my father is my father.
Daddy, still I wake
on that broken throne of gnarled torsos.
Daddy, the dark power you cast
I took.

Though sometimes still
the girl curls
into your humped darkness
contorts her fishy body
into the great heartsea
beneath your ribs

and in silence
works her way all the way back
to an old woman coming from Asia
and further than that
to an old white whale
cruising the pelvis of the world

until our story (You, the ruthless boy
so young even still
I see you outlive me

is turning into
foam
and the great birth
from your severed and flung
genital.

L.A. Blonde

—For barry eisenberg, who, finding a photograph of me at sixteen as
a beauty queen riding down Main Street on the hood of a baby blue
Thunderbird, said, "God, Sharon, you have a lot of karma to work out."

Something of the light on sage there,
the light exploding off the ocean.
Something of the burning light pouring onto the hills,
hurling back down the canyons as flame.
And the beautiful stars running into the light,
and the beautiful stars running out of the light
from reeling earthquake, live oak,
and the rampage of ice plant.

Shadow and light
of the groundswells, the highways and beaches
washed clean by Santa Ana, hot
Grandmother of God and hard rains
in an hour, the danger then
in the dry beds of flash flood,
the swollen arroyos
that undermine every house in the foothills.
The danger then of the city
pushing you off
into the unwatered desert.

The way on winter days
it's almost light enough
to photograph something like
angels in the eucalyptus, the one hundred
varieties, and hummingbirds,
symbol of resurrection, hovering
the cacti gardens.
And high over the bird of paradise,
palm and poinsettia,
vulture
that only light has blinded

to the secret
of bougainvillaea.

Marilyn Monroe said she was always running into
other people's unconsciouses.
You lift the hand from the pale ice of your gown
to the dark electricity of air.
The sun heats the hood, turns your shoulders red.
You wave along the collective stare lining the boulevard.
In the blinding light they appear
like a negative risen from solution,
the skin black,
the eyes, hair, teeth, and nails,
as they roar *Blondie!*
bleached out.

Love Song for a Man Whose Mother Killed Herself

Your open mouth like the ocean
where you allow me, swimming.
Beneath all things, the Bible says
are the waters
but men don't open this way.
They are the ships headed for some horizon, the rescuers

dragging the lake for days for her body, you said.

You have opened yourself so wide
you are the water your mother drowned in.
She lies at the bottom of you,
the dark deep water that covers you.

I see her face sleeping with open eyes
looking toward the sun.
I am wanting

the secret of this watery garden
the secret the leaves hide
and the wind
call it the world
the secret she would not live without.

It is deep going between here and the new country.
In the night we are seen waving back to the shore.
Voices call for us. I emerge
over your body to see the earth in light.

You have opened to me.
You are the first man who has ever opened to me.
Somehow you have made yourself

the man she would not live without.

from Visions of a Daughter of Albion

1. LAND OF HEART'S DESIRE

I sleep beneath a map of my country
and dream she is loving her body
out of political boundaries
I hear her crying
what is this place to me
if you are lost?

Now I sleep beneath America
Sacajawea leading Lewis and Clark across the uncharted world

Prairie grass so high mounted soldiers are lost

Waiting days for mile-wide buffalo herds
to cross in front of you

Now I sleep beneath America
and pull white men from the prohibitive world
deeper into my wilderness
and the promise of sexual love

Cherokees across miles of my flesh
Redwood trees that never die

I am ploughing North America
the night that is our history
the Body we must put our bodies up against

O, but you are dreaming me she cries
because she knows
bloodlines that have been lost
and blood
that has so soaked

the frontier and all the lands left behind
her soul can find
no well of clear water

My Mother Is a Poem I Will Never Write ✓

He couldn't wait to meet my mother.
He kept saying you'll never know
who your woman is
until you meet her mother.
He said it so often he angered me, he, a safe
orphan, with his mother self-drowned

But I think he must see me
as she is walking in this light
down from her home to meet us,
an orphan herself, but as clear
as anything on this Oregon coast.
Even I can feel myself as she comes,
carried in that wide house between her hips.

My mother is a poem I'll never be able to write
though everything I write is a poem to my mother

of whom he later said as we were leaving
And your mother, oh, your mother
Deep. Deep water. The waters run deep.

Kerouac and Monroe on Kalaloch

1.

Long ago they found each other here.
She wanted to be like the wild stallion
she had seen in Nevada. He had lost his mind
in Massachusetts.

They sat all day on the long beach.
They drank beer propped against drowned trees.
Sometimes they spoke. Mostly
they stared at the sea. Low tide. High.
Their famous faces flared on the screen of the sky.
Their faces grew tired, turned red.
Their limbs dried. The sun fell. They became
driftwood. They were dying. She said
tell me of sex.

He recited Rilke's Ninth Elegy.
She heard only the line
and escapes
in ecstasy
beyond the violin.
Tell me, she cried, of when
you were a kid.

2.

She slid her hand down the haggard belly, held him.
He was warm. He stirred. He stayed small.
He slept. She watched twelve pelicans
row the horizon. She laid her head
on the blade of his shoulder.

She saw his face above the waves.
It was the saddest face she had ever seen.
She saw the face held knowledge

of her death. She saw the man
might be the man
who murders her.

They walked miles up the beach
looking for a bed.
He quoted poets who had slept here.
He said he knew the island was Tatoosh
from the poems. He said poets
find their lovers here. Later
they found a road sign. It named the island
Destruction.

    3.

In a tavern on the highway an Indian was saying
Hunting elk is a disease. I seen
an elk hunter pump seven bullets
into an elk that wasn't there.
And he didn't even have
his gun.

Tell me about sex, she said
as they drank. Tell me
who you are. He said, I've been
ruthless.

The bartender asked, Where you two from?
You look familiar, like a couple I know
in Wyoming. The Indian went on
You can take any road out of here,
sleep over night, hear them
the mating calls, cougar, lynx, black bear
this time of year.

They walked back through slashpiles.
It was dark. He said
I learned to be ruthless

from the Church. I took
a vow of poverty.

She searched the sky for the southern stars.
She saw how far she had come.
Shit. She said, I was born
in L.A.

    4.

They made a bed beneath Cedar
on a bluff above the sea.
She would have preferred the beach.
He was afraid of rain.
She was glad to know
of something he felt.

They made a small fire.
They cooked soup in the can.
They covered themselves with a single blanket.

    5.

When first they loved
when her body lifted off the needles
when her body rose and churned like the demonic waves
when her cries, lifted to the night,
screamed back at them like gulls

she knew why
no man
had ever stayed with her.

    6.

When second they fucked, she sobbed.
She screamed. It was not
pleasure. He folded his arms around her back,
lifted her from the ground.
The water rolled from her face. He said
What is my name?

7.

When they loved again she remembered
this may be the man who kills me.
She felt his hands
form the body she knew as a girl.
She saw the raccoons watching them.
In stars' light their needles glistened.
She thought
Cougar. Lynx. Black Bear

and such a light body he laid on her
So thin. His ribs. He was hard to find.
He fled more than she. Are you ever . . .
she searched Cedar for the word
Emotional. When he was through
he poured his dark face into her pale hair.
She felt his body heave
in the attempt to cry.

8.

She watched the Virgin slip into the water.
She woke him. Tell me about
Ruthless.

He told her. She lay quiet. This man
could kill her. She watched
the Scales of Love go down.
She woke him. She whispered
don't be ruthless
with me. You can get
whatever you want
without being
Ruthless.

He promised. He slept. Of course, she said
to the Scorpion, I can
take it. He was awake. He said
I know you can.

9.

Once from the night she heard the Indian again.
Wednesday is hump night. That's halfway
over the hump. She saw the raccoons
getting ready. Cougar. Black Bear. She said
Ruthless means
a promise
is nothing.

He was awake. He said
I know. I thought of that.

10.

When again they loved, as the Hunter
drowned, as the night rolled over
the hump of the sun, he shook her shoulders
and cried, Do you even
know my name?

11.

In the silver light of morning, at the coldest hour
they loved again. The tide was high. Water
rushed the bluff. Cedar flared above them.
He buried his mouth
in the wild yellow grass
between her legs.
The seasons changed. It was summer
when they met. Now the trees flamed
and fell.

12.

He took his shirt from her.
He leaned over the bluff.
The sky and sea found his body
for her. Tell me, she said,
about sex.

He put on his black leather cap.
The saddest face she had ever seen
smiled. He said, My name is Jack.
Your name is Marilyn.
And that is why we sojourn here
alone on Kalaloch.

13.

They are so far from home.
She says his name. He touches her lips.
She will escape into ecstasy beyond the violin.
When he can't cry, he will see his own face
above the waves, he will shoot
fictitious elk, he will be without his
gun. He will be ruthless.

Crazy Horse

1.

I dream he is my lover.
We lie on the hard ground beneath a single robe, the marriage blanket.
We lie against an old wooden fort on the dark prairie.
Inside, men drink as in a lighted bar.
Across the black night I feel the others pressing in on us.
Against the black night I feel him beside me, hard and lean.
Then I feel him out there, coming, naked on his horse.

2.

In my oldest dream on earth I am shooting and shooting.
The small revolver blooms into red-hot and yellow flames
that disappear from me across the ravished nightland.
When he is beside me, dark and lean, he shows me how to shoot
to save his life. There are times when I am alone and know
he is trying to come to me out of the black night.
I hold off the others who crawl across the field to kill us.

1.

He is not like any man I have known.
He takes me all the way into the male world.
There is no separation as with other men with women.
Our survival depends on each other.
He is the one I have waited for, my strange,
familiar Oglala.

2.

I'm shooting into the night as they crawl across the field
to kill us. I seek him among the rifles.
When the black fog lifts, I see him afoot, surrounded.
I pull him on the back of my horse and zigzag back
through the soldiers, the burning-red bullets.

1.

Beneath the black marriage shawl our clear bodies lie naked on the ground.
We are invisible. I braid grass stems into his light hair.
There are streakings all about us, arrows and lead balls,
but they disappear before hitting us. The danger is great
only if we fail each other. Through the whole night
a chorus of wolves resounds from the frozen mountains around us.
Beneath our massive robe we lie in the deep ease of each's body.
The dark. And the dark ground.

2.

On the Holy Road he has left sticks pointing in the direction he has gone.
There I find him on the ridge above the dwindling buffalo herd,
his gun silent across his knees, watching, as if he is herding his cattle.
When he sees me coming up the long hill our eyes lock.
Behind him the storm cloud of night rolls, and thunder stirs the hair
about his waist. He starts toward me well forward on his horse
whose neck is high, whose feet move freely. I see the splattering
of hail spots on his naked body that makes him invisible to the others.
Only the hair about his waist and the heel fringes of his moccasins
stir as he rides to me.

1.

He takes the rope of the horse from my hand
and swings his blanket about me, holding me in its folds.
He presses the wet zigzag lightning of his face against my cheek.
I put my hand beneath his large testicles. I hold him.

We lean against the hard lean night, the enemy shadows all around us.
He is the first man who lets me love him as deeply as I know.
We lie on our sides facing each other beneath the heavy black shawl.
Our heads almost touch the unpainted building of the prairie.
In this way we join our bodies. There is no separation.
With my free hand I play with the small, brown stone behind his ear.

He lies in me long, searching quietly, as with a free hand, a deep and great
   place.
I stir on him slowly, rising upwards, as through a flood.

He becomes a part of what is there, a hard, gold depth.
Behind his face the small red hawk flies, making his *killy-killy* crying.
Without quickening his pace, moving deeply, deliberately, he listens,
this violet-dark son who has been killed and shines no more.
My crazy Oglala, my strange animal.

2.

He comes out of the dark purple night, naked on his horse
but for the splattering of painted hailstones, the lightning streak down
   his face.
As he comes he fires the prairie, burning the grass the soldiers' horses
need to live, filling every clear day with great rolling clouds of smoke,
the sun, blood-red, the nightsky shining as from northern lights.
I will grieve through seven generations for this sexual lover,
this sleeper on the ground. The nightearth beneath me is his body.
I cannot answer all the bright heat of the sun, most men
with their inward meanness.
He is the strange, heavy man who goes with me.
When we lie together on the ground
I am careful not to hold his arms down.

Infant Found Alive at Wounded Knee

1.

Something lifts me from her
once a warm bath I lay in,
now who shudders in a great blow
that goes through me, then grows cold.

The white river I suck from her
turns to red, bitter blood.
A heavy snow begins to fall.

Under the blue starlit tepee of night
I can see them
beneath the drifting snow,
huddled heaps, scattered bundles and clots.

When the sun returns
ice slashes me like knives
glistening red
in the morning light.

The wind comes up and I become
a frozen knot
that will never be untied.

2.

I ride in his arm on horseback
across the blinding world.
He is a man who sees things
that make his body shudder
worse than hers.
He cries *wounded*, our knees
are gone now. His tears
fall on me, a warm thaw.

Later he says
Open your mouth.
We have no choice.
I will let down the milk for you
from the father river
of my breasts. What we are
is what we are. Why else
would I have them?

I name you
Little Mocking Bird
for life.

Appalachian Song

I see a dirt road inside myself and on it I am walking.
At the far end where the sun is setting
are my children, all the western scattering
of my flesh.

Here are the voices I hear, the unaccountable melancholy,
the dark hearts of my grandparents, storied in my flesh.
When I look to the hills I hear
shattering like glass, the red of the loam
soaked from me.

Near the cabin at the clearing's center
a mournful Scottish melody.
When I walk amidst the flowering dogwood
a thousand tongues lift their words to me

Call my name in the act of love. I am full of loss
and the shadowy Cherokee. At night I fall
into our migrations, settlers drifting across
the Great Barrier.

The cold winters you say, the loss of war paint,
the images tattooed on the skin of my brain.
My daughter in the river we drink, its body
lifting her before she knew the body of a man.

When you call me, your face, bald as the eroded hills,
is blessedly here, between me and these scenes.
But when we ride the boy in your scrotum, which stores,
like glass, the ruins of this place, you pull
houses full of blood, mountains full of smoke, down
on top of me.

from Ramon: The Colorado

12. MOJAVE

The nightsky rises and blows
the riverine call of nightingale.
Joshua, bathed in moon, beckons me
to the high horizon.

Blind Orion runs in place
to catch his eyes in the falling sun
while the comet falls through him
heavy and swift as the songs of the daughters
calling from the old reedboats on the river.

I move into his grotesque arms, carefully turn
within the hairy thorns, the moon's shaft,
to face the east, the land I've just traversed.

A red mist rises off the dry riverbed.
A lizard humps, bunches at my feet.
The border falls away to cloud, sky,
an old woman geographer dreaming
Colorado, so wide, so deep, passing
without sound.

And suddenly it is you,
O, my majesty,
playing with me, humming
through your vegetable arms.

from

PSYCHE DRIVES
THE COAST
1990

Sometimes I have to sleep
In dangerous places, on cliffs underground
Walls that still hold the whole prints
of ancient ferns.

—JAMES WRIGHT

and laughing they went away
deep so deep
into narrative

—SUSAN HOWE

To live outside the law
you gotta be honest

—BOB DYLAN

Earlier than lust, not plain,
Behind a darkened face of memory,
My inner animal revives.
Beware, that I am tame.
Beware philosophies
Wherein I yield.

—LAURA RIDING

Outlaw

1.

Don't shoot. I've
eaten this country
alive

Your hard male body, like a road, I drove
your famous miles, back of vans
low on backseats

The states grow out of me now
The borders are my skin
The fatal flag flies, tattooed
between my hips

The hum of my motor
blends with the thump of little bodies
and the static rockbeat
of my radio

and I am gone
like the semen you spilt to the ground
when you fantasized me a whore
and then would not love me
for fear I was a whore

2.

Everyone was looking for me
I was always right here
a mute piece of music
a deep down motion
running through your blood

Don't shoot
In the windows of all your houses

my face is printed
where I pressed it to glass

she

who robbed her father's banks

3.

Crowds on the streets at night looking for me
But I was caught
in the dancer's grace of apple trees
in cold country
I never lived before

Don't shoot, who
could recognize me now?
There's a dead man
hanging
in the middle of my forehead
His cold charred body
emerges
from my cunt and anus
My mouth expels
a new country

4.

And so I walked away in my rich white skin
while you scattered all your parts to the wind

I picked up your hand
your hand without fingers
by the winter waters

and placed it on my breasts

you were still warm
I called your name
You did not answer

So I'm gone
like the semen you spilt on the ground
when you wanted me a whore

and then could not love me
for fear I was a whore

    5.

I am a woman
a traveler back and forth

I joined the army
traveling back and forth
across the continent

the sun coming up
the sun going down
the stars planted in their routes

the dancer's grace of apple trees
in cold country
I never lived before

I learned constellations, windrows,
rotations of farmers' land
food for the people
and the ache of you

the fucking ache of you

What does it take
to communicate?
The words burnt deep in my flesh

burn a gory road before me
the only escape

6.

Everyone was looking for me
I was always right here

Once I camped in a national park
with a caravan of retired people
At night inside their little campers
their blue phosphorescent lights
served me up for dinner, a cold cold burn

this is your daughter
this is your daughter

Everyone
was afraid
I was
their daughter

7.

I am the woman alone on the road at night
you catch in your headlights
Afraid, you do not stop

I walk the middle of the world
with a child at each side
another tied in a scarf on my back

Tonight we will sleep in a cold open field
I will lay my hands on its heart

I will blanket them with pine needles
I will hear the screech and groan of wagon wheels
I will pull dead Indians from the soil

I will be thankful I have not house or land
I will be thankful I have no money

I am a woman
I walk in the middle of the world
I follow the cross of the gypsy trail
over the world and back

8.

I went down to the bottom of the mountains
I went down to the sea in your scrotum
I rode out the dark untried eggs

I saw the body and soul are one
I saw when the body fragments
so does the soul

I saw that in death our parts
are strewn and scattered

piece of flesh, piece of soul

and our tortured lament
is our parts
crying to one another
across the ever-widening
abyss

9.

I am only a mother
trying to piece together
a child

10.

I am a woman
a traveler back and forth

When I knelt to your groin the first time
and took you in my mouth
I felt the fish beat

for the cold pull
of the distant sea

and when I took you in my mouth
I was the moon receiving
your wondrous light

now I am scattered like stars
you spilt
on the ground

   11.

I was held down

My clitoris was cut out
with the broken neck of a bottle
and thrown in the dirt

           I am your clitoris   *no.*
           singing in the throats of little sparrows

I was held down

My foetus was cut out
and thrown in the sewer

                I am your daughter
                I was saved by the water
                that threw me on the shore
                I was raised by the wolves
                I belong to No Man's Land

I was held down

My breasts were cut off
and thrown over the Rockies
I tattooed on my scars

a heart with an arrow
plunged all the way through

        I am your breast
        thrust up as the Rockies
        Arrowheads, mining shafts
        and mineral hot springs
        are lost deep in my folds

I am gone
into the dark activity beneath your skin
and come up through you
that in caves of history
the boy becoming king
dreams

I am a woman
a traveler back and forth
I belong to No Man's Land
who hung my torso
from every post

and filled all my small holes
with rocks

   12.

I hold my womb in my hands
its ever-living population
I will never have children
They must rise in me

The Present Living Body

   13.

I made love to a woman in the Rockies
a prayer in the middle of the world
We rolled back and forth

across the native soil
the flesh of Pocahontas
while under us
old gods jacked off

14.

My crimes are many
I loved a Mojave boy
and dreamed every night
I impregnated him

I am a streetwalker
I lie down with all of you
I take you in my body
The more you fuck me
the less you know me

I am the 9 million witches
you burned at the stake
Now I am back, bounding over these states
From pole to pole across the hills I move
into every house
I change my clothes in each one
I am your daughter

I am every furtive fantasy
you've ever had
I am your left hand

15.

I am the lissome young girl
who captivated the gaze
of all those who saw me

You were clenched and breathless
as we went down
and I took you
deep inside

Many ghosts were colored lights
the aurora borealis
raining, tumbling, roaring
chasing years across the sky

When I took you in my mouth
I was the moon
receiving the light
that lit our tent
and morning that waited
at the end of the world

Now I am Crazy Jane
I will leap from my grave
when you walk by

I vanished long ago

gone like semen spilt on the ground
gone like last year's wild roses

like the hot stars you carry in your little sacks
like the hot stars trailing from your mouth

gone like morning at the end of the world

like the sun risen halfway to noon
and then falling back to dawn

"And the lonely psyche goes up thru the
boy to the King that in the caves of history
dreams."
—ROBERT DUNCAN, "A POEM BEGINNING
   WITH A LINE BY PENDAR"

Concert

You pull me across the sun to the stage
The eighty thousand in the thousand hills behind us
push me forward to the stage, the driving rockbeat pleas
of the musicians begging please back up you'll crush us
begging please come up and fuck us

I dreamt I was blue and so I was opened
They drew out my heart and placed here instead
the martyred crowd, Bonnie crying *I'm blowing away*
and shadows
keep taking my love

to our feet, a miracle, we make room
a couple begging please take these chains, the beat of his ass
plunging her deeper into white trash, the deep
South, a boy turning his back on the guitars
to show us his face, colored scarves
of napalm, defoliated stone

Drums beat the blue skinscape of graves shelved above the town
the Purple Heart embroidered on his levi jacket
As we roar down the front wave of electricity, Breath
expiring from us seeds onto the hills, he stares
at me, he hums

      what is it or was it
      and what will it ever be¿

                  —*For Bonnie Raitt, Stompin 76, Galax, Virginia*

The Stations of the Cross

Jesus is a frail sorrowing girl.
Her 12-foot hands are too large, they must be carried by another.
They lift, as she walks, her pink-floral, old-lace gown
and patchwork quilt that keeps the cold out.
Around her neck is tied
a man's orange-plaid tie and from her waist
2 flashlights, a can of pork and beans, spoon and fork, a plate with her
face on it   clanging and banging as she walks   Jesus is

a hobo, a junk man
a blackbottom coffee pot hangs between his legs, it
is difficult to walk with baggies of water
hanging off your wrists, your huge
head, your extra pair of socks drying on your violin, your bow
of broken twigs and old string, Jesus is

the Bride of Spring   she wears a new
tuxedo over her soiled wedding gown and her old shoes follow
yearningly the Giant Fish of a Cross
wafting through the room   wagging its big head in the rafters

and he falls trying to carry it,
a tree that keeps turning into a woman on his back   who cries
will he rise¿   Jesus

is a small trembling boy who must have help to carry it, Jesus
is standing before his Mother, he
sets the table, he will make her coffee.
His body is growing tiny wings and Veronica
a famous star, so wealthy, so beautiful
wipes the Lake from his face
and he gives it up   into her hands, falling as the women cry

and will he rise¿   and will he rise¿   and will he rise¿   Jesus is

stripped of his garments, he is after all a
bony old woman nailed to the Fish
whose scales cut her thin skin, whose penis is broken
twigs   and old string
whose soft belly stretches and moans
for you, my mind she is crying is trying to tell it
to follow

a 12-foot stuffed puppet with blood and the lame
tied to its waist
who prays at my feet   who drums their tin cans

and will she rise? and will she rise? and will she   rise? am I born
to die?   to lay my body down and lose? I can hear

many confusing conversations between the stained glass fragments of
    my body
floating East and West and North and South
and my legs which are pushing down through the clouds, this Evil
Ceiling   and many women are here
beholding from afar   my raggedy tragedy
singing

and did I rise?   and I did rise?   and did I
rise?

—*Good Friday, 3–4 p.m., April 8, 1977, Albion, California, for
    The Bread and Puppet Theater, Plainfield, Vermont, 1974*

from The Orpheus Poems

ELECTRIC VIOLIN

I was dead wood
forsaken on a wall
like a difficult fiddle
without music

as you said
the day you met me
you took it off a wall
years it hadn't been played
years you hadn't played

You bent yourself to me
in just this shocking manner
a new way with an old song
your hands flying
root and stem light volts
to my water
and pumped
with astounding precision
a tune
the terror and beauty
from me

Eros ✓

All day the sea makes moan
and throws itself against the land.
This is not the wind, you say,
this is the water
throwing itself
from Japan.

All day the water throws itself
from side to side around the world.
The radio tells of beaches
torn in the Carolinas,
Gulf of Mexico
and down in
Los Angeles.

All day our love makes moan
and I am a young girl
in the heavy moaning sea
I swam in before I knew
the body of a man.

When I knew the body of a man
I never again went into the sea.
But now I know when you are gone
and I am old
and lovers come no more

I will take my body again
into the deep moaning sea

Beneath the World:
Two Poems to the Child Never to be Born

1.

I sleep beneath a map of the world.
The world glows in the dark.
In the furthest place
the Northern Lights
bear down.

In the morning I will bear down.
This thing. This fish
swollen in the seas, glowing
beneath love.

Canada and Alaska yearn over me
for the Orient. China, as if in flight,
flees the map. You must walk
south from the dead center, the U.S.
The eyes, the heart, the feet
must follow
the drift to the east, antipodes,
Tierra del Fuego: the delicate
fire in this painting.

O, island. O little land
I see your journey
on my water's swift current.

Tomorrow I will open.
The axis will tilt, the earth will quake

and he and I
two lonely gods
will suck you
from gravity.

But I hear, little spirit,
your suck,
the great song
Corazon.
Your heart
and the world glows.
Corazon blue, corazon red,
corazon negra.

   2.

Tomorrow I'll break

I'll forsake
words altogether I will paint
with my soul
the curvature
of Earth, the tipping of her
axis, her wobbly
pole

this pale face, this series of faces
that comes now
a spermy cloud
to cover Her

I will spend my life walking
your borders
these land masses broken
for you, these continents
and their drift

I will wash you in the great mourning
in the great morning sea
of the East Pacific Rise

I will lose you
in the nightsea
of the Mid-Atlantic Ridge

You will be unknown
in the West Wind Drift

from **Self**

> We go out into the world to find our face.
> —RAINER MARIA RILKE

10. The Meaning of No Self

I hide
my face, the front of my body
too yin

shot through
by spears of light
The universe bears down
to get through

my shoulders

stooped, my head
feathers

> At my sex my left hand holds
> the structure
> that holds the sun
>
> I am overlit, over
> exposed. The three-headed dog
> yelps and dances
> at my heels
> I am dread
>
> penetrated
> by wheat

—For Diane di Prima, the Hermit card

from PART II. PSYCHE DRIVES THE COAST

2. "It don't mean a thing if it ain't got that swing" (Bertoldt Brecht)

In a lounge in Seaside she takes shelter
in the music of her parents.
She walks into their darkness, a theatre.
Their eyes keep to the screen of her body.

It's true. She sees it too.
She's lived the great tragedies of their time.
Sometimes she can't change fast enough.
The bartender bends to her, *honey*
then reels. A woman

is a sometimes thing. Wanders
into the wrong room. Her parents'
bedroom as a child. He asks her
to marry him, saying *the deep
anguish in your eyes
speaks pages*

of dialogue. But it grows
dark. Fishing lights bob way out.
Her husbands signaling her, who might
know her. One more tune at their windows, she lets go
a girl crying in their arms. Then leaves

her face behind. Goes back out.
The sea loud.
Goes down the road.

3. Sleep: The I in Language

The deer startled
as if by cedar and
my light

the stillness.   the water.   the light
the enormity of being, these trees
their trunks. My womb
turns over
the quiet. the dark. the density.   the depth

the presence.   the dark.   the light
in the density of the forest

my body contracts. Turns over

    a million stories. A million
    Is
    in the proud waters

    of Loulan
    the hands of men

    inside

5. The God Comes Out of Your Mouth, California

A half moon so large at the play.
We are thankful it's not full
over the ominous land. Said.
It's all turning to. She
writing so still

Meditation of the world's vast Memory.
Then the waters overwhelmed us.
The stream had gone over our soul.
We are thankful it's not full
over the land of Love.
This myth. Almost said. it's purple. turning
political

Then the political waters had gone over our soul
over this loving land, turning
purple so still

It's death to souls to become water
but our soul is escaped as a bird
out of our mouths. Solidifies
his Castle high in the Empyrean, Hearst
printing the myths   these

Cows of Heaven, the most
pelicans I've ever seen

prehistoric purple on the currents of each

other and the wave, uncovered
in the prehistoric city of Loulan   some ancient
minority, enormous throats of Blondie in her piety
graying the troughs of the northern rim

Meditation on the world's vast Memory . . .
—SUSAN HOWE

from Hunger

*—Written during a twelve-day fast in support of the political prisoners on
hunger strike in Maze Prison, Ireland, May 1981*

from HUNGER II

The World and Francis Hughes

Now this rush into air, now into this fine
line of bone and dust, now this maze,
vacuum and fog of the North Sea, this
one eye closing the world
that rots the skin

Now this 16 again, this birthday party.
The girl bends, kisses your chest.
You fly home on the old road
having seen the world

to this police check, this question of
God, your answer as innocent
as the blows
again and again
to the part of your body
just coming
to sacred knowledge.

Now into the small room you are placed.
This bed of your parents, bed of your conception,
this only world for months, hurt and this
question.
The books your father brings you from the library,
now this history. When you are born
again into the world you will *find out*
for yourself, each step
sharp pain, a limp

into the moment of the accused
the political act
this dream
a solitary young man
Osian! Cuchulain! Frankie
The Unvanquished! descending
the world the paratroopers storm
this moment of scourge, fire and sun
and bodies like matches
disintegrating to clover.

Now it is not possible
to introduce food
into the body
that has lived its dreams.

Your brother approaches the world
you lie upon, a weeping shadow
reeling off from the stench
of your blackening flesh
Now

rush into air, bring
the moldy lips
to his ear, say from Compassion
the only world

> *"Not to worry brother.*
> *It all began*
> *with a kiss on the heart."*

from HUNGER III: THE DAYS

Day Eleven: Hunger Songs

> And what if excess of love
> Bewildered them till they died?
> —YEATS, "EASTER 1916"

the beauty of the light
here, how the body
must work

to bring food to it
to come to this world
we must, so large
already in it

to simply stay

here

~

we are so fat
with the light
we hate

I spend all week
writing "The Pornographer"

the Father who refuses to bring his Body
into the world
this too green

The Olympic Mountains rise up
shatter the light
the islands in the Strait
too real   shatter

the word

~

I want my song
to go out
over the world
the way his hand
came over my face
that morning
in sleep

I am thankful
it's not me
in the Ireland
Maze
I'd be One
vowed to the Chain

but I wouldn't
want
to lose

this world

~

Night after night I hunger
for an old love, hunger
for Something I cannot say, I don't
understand   I see
the many fragments of his hard brown face
thrown in with the pieces
broken from my heart

I work and work
the poem   Something
I don't know
will ever be read

like his hand
over my face asleep

this 4 a.m.
before leaving
for work

~

The body cannot just be
but must make, must
work
(every minute

food
into it

over and over
across the world
to simply stay
to even enter
so small
we are
in it

Night after night I ache
to be
intimate
with it   Hunger
for something
I cannot see
I wake to the many fragments
of myself
thrown everywhere
(this morning before work
              the islands

              we are

                    so fat
day after day
I eat
the pornographer whose son

cannot come
into   his Body
       this too green   this
       too lit

The Olympics rise up
the islands in the Strait beneath
shatter

        Love

       cannot just be
       but must make
       a perfect body

In the beginning was the Word
Now my Body
cannot just Be
but must make
the World
to stay apart
from it

must put
the World into it
to make

day after day

the Son

       who refuses the Father
these Ones
who give the Body

       this 4 a.m. when He rose
       to work
       on *The Straits*

fragments
too lit

by a Kiss   on the Heart

these islands

I can't
eat

the Sun
an old son

purest
most lovely

of mirrors

I squint

into

from HUNGER IV

End Hunger

The Day That Charles And Diane Married Kevin Lynch Died On His 69th
Day Without Food. On Her Honeymoon Flight To Gibraltar The New
Princess Of Wales Vacuumed The Carpet While The Eighth IRA Prisoner
Kieran Doherty Fasted To Death On His 73rd Day Without Food

*On September 13 the hunger strike by Irish nationalists in Maze Prison ended,
reportedly because of pressure exerted by the mothers of the prisoners.*

> *Too long a sacrifice*
> *Can make a stone of the heart.*

> I write it out in a verse—
> MacDonagh and MacBride
> And Connolly and Pearse
> Now and in time to be,
> Whenever green is worn,
> Are changed, changed utterly:
> A terrible beauty is born.
> —YEATS, "EASTER, 1916"

May 5: Bobby Sands, 27, his 66th day without food
May 11: Bob Marley, 31, "them belly full but we hungry"
May 12: Frankie Hughes, 27, his 59th day without food
May 21: Raymond McCreesh, 24, his 61st day without food
May 22: Patrick O'Hara, 24, his 61st day without food
July 8: Joe McDonnel, 30, his 61st day without food
July 13: Martin Hurson, 25, his 45th day without food
August 1: Kevin Lynch, 25, his 69th day without food
August 3: Kieran Doherty, 25, his 73rd day without food
August 9: Tom McElwee, 23, his 62nd day without food
August 9: Michael Devine, 20, his 60th day without food

Ground Zero

1.

We met on an evening in July
in one of the old taverns of this town,
two poets, unable to write, newly arrived,
hunted and haunted. For me,
the escape. For you,
the return.

You said you would show me
the Olympic Peninsula.

The road was overgrown.
In the headlights of your car I cleared the trees.
The cabin was vandalized, gutted,
the twenty-six oddshaped windows
opening onto the Strait, the Sound, Canada, and all the northern sky
shot out. The sink, the pump, the stoves,
even the doors, stolen.
You wandered around, then out to the deck,
seeming to forget me in the debris.

Victoria, the only human light,
shimmered on the foreign shore.
I heard the groan of a fishing boat below the bluff,
a strange cry from the woods, like a woman,
your ex-wife, the children.

We lay on a narrow mattress in the loft,
amidst bullet shells, beer cans, mold and glass,
the cold, hard bed of delinquent teenagers.

The moon was a broken boat through the bullet-shattered skylight.
We told each other.
First words. I said
one night stand. You said ground zero.
I said I lost my children, my lover.

You said submarine, fucking vandals.
I said kids with no place to go, kids forbidden
to love. You said holocaust. Apocalypse.
I pulled you over on me. The volcano erupted.
The world turned to ash. I cried
love cannot be gutted.
The moon, the stars, the giant trees watched
through a bullet hole.

2.

You moved in, installed sink, stoves, water pump.
Sixty oddshaped windows. You sat here
pissed as the eagle that stared from the bluff,
the grease pen numbers on the glass around your brooding head
like kabbalah, some secret military code.
When I visited, I felt a vandal.
When I left you cried deserted.
Betrayed.

In November I moved in.
Sheetrock. Yellow paint named Sunlight.
My white dog, Moonlight.
I said I'd stay until the place
became a landscape in my dreams.
By moon's light through the bullet hole
I began to write.
Your words: The Duckabush. The Dosewallips. The Hamma Hamma.

It snowed in December.
You followed Coyote's tracks to the log where he slept.
A trapper came on the deep path.
He had Coyote. He gave you his card.
He boasted he'd get the rest.
He hinted that for money he could get them for you.

You were not easy to love.
You couldn't speak. Your tongue was cut out.
I left, screaming down the interstate,
avoiding the road over the mountains

to my old, equally beautiful, home.
You wrote me. One Trident submarine equals
two thousand and forty Hiroshimas.

In the cities I was weighted with cedar, an inland sea,
like provisions carried on my back.
Friends I'd always respected said
they couldn't live without culture.
I was weighted with the culture of eagle, coyote, people
like weather, like stars, functions of nature, not
human will, money, concrete.

   3.

I came back to study the language of gulls,
the stories they scream to each other
as they fly off their sanctuary,
Protection Island.

You pulled me up the stairs.
Beyond your head I watched the moon through the bullet hole.
You said six layers of mountains
from the road, you said rivers
without end. You quoted Rilke's
Neptune of the blood and his terrible trident.
You said Trident
Submarine. You said
zero.

I came back to stare back at Eagle,
to cut, carry, and chop our firewood,
to piss in the tall fern, to defecate
in the first little house you ever built.
I came back and broke my habit at last
of the electric typewriter.
I came back to our cruel and grinding poverty,
never enough kerosene, gasoline, postage, paper or pens.
We quit filling the propane. It is so cold in our house
the little food on our shelves is naturally iced.

I came back to listen to the woods,
gull squawk and moan dance of cedar, fir and alder,
the high scream of wind through the mouth of Haro,
Rosario, Deception Pass
where the ships disappear on the inward passage.
I came back to listen to your breath
as you sleep beside me. Poet. Your words.
Puma. Ish. Milosz. The children
who once lived here.

    4.

You weighted me with your poems,
like provisions. I left, drove home.
My children were grown, gone.
Your words pulled me back.

We climb the stairs together.
The roof leaks, the cabin is for sale.
I say it is ours for now. Our one night stand,
our two hundred nights.

You tell me of this thing that is coming,
the deadliest weapon ever made.
Two football fields, four stories high.
Two thousand and forty Hiroshimas.

It can be anywhere in the world, undetected,
and hit its target within half a foot.
It can be anywhere in the world and no one,
not the President, not the Computer
will be able to find it.

One day soon it will enter the Strait of Juan de Fuca.
The most evil thing ever created
will float beneath our cabin, then down
the Hood Canal.

You say four hundred and eight cities
from a single submarine. You say

First Strike Weapon. You say
shoot our their silos. You say
USS *Ohio*.

    5.

I came upon an old man
teaching his granddaughter and grandson
how to shoot.

I sat here alone.
The door banged open and four kids
burst in. Perfume, six packs, party clothes.
I think I frightened them
as much as they frightened me.

On clear days the islands rise up.
San Juan. Lopez. Orcas, white skyscrapers
on Vancouver. How many ships, my love,
have come and gone since we came? How many whales,
eagles, coyotes and gulls?
I finished my epic poem here.
You finished *The Straits*.

Every night the human city
shimmers and beckons on the Canadian shore.
Every night of one whole week
the sky wove and unwove
the rainbow flags of all the north
delicately over us. The aurora
borealis.

Two seasons of snow, now the season of light again.
My one night stand, our four hundred
nights.

I saw car lights descend Protection Island
to the water.
The leaks in the roof washed away
my nightwritten words.

We saw six killer whales
rise and fall through the water.
You said my rejected poems. I said
your small-minded editors. I said
I can almost understand now
what the gulls are saying.

6.

My dreams take place on an inland sea,
a land soaked in silver shadows and blue.
We are traveling to the heart of the continent.
We are looking for a room to rent. We are having a baby.
We are building a house.

You say unrecognized. Unpublished. I say just
wait. You say holocaust. You say apocalypse. I say
love.

Once you went with me.
Once you came for me.

We climb the loft together. This, you say
is your home now. This northwest corner. This last place
we can run

this bed of outlaws, circle of mountains, finger
of glacier water, dark sun of winter behind
Mt. Olympus.

7.

Light shoots through the skylights.
Twenty full moons wake us.
Moonlight sleeps below by the fire, cries from nightmare.
The Manx, the Siamese watch us through the bullet hole.
We lie in terror,
watch the giant trees arch and blow over us,
rain and wind so fierce
we wait without words to be crushed.

Finally I say maybe we should leave. You say
where would we go?
You say death like a storm that might or might not
blow over. You say Puma.
I say Tatoosh means Thunderbird.
Like Phoenix, like rebirth.

You say the last crisis is not death,
but how to be beautiful.
How to die
beautifully.

8.

Say the word Hiroshima.
Reflect on its meaning for one second.
Say and understand Hiroshima again.
Say and understand Hiroshima two thousand and forty times.

Assuming you are able to understand Hiroshima
in one second, you will be able to understand Trident
in thirty-four minutes. That's one Trident submarine.
To understand the destructive power of the whole
Trident fleet, it will take you seventeen hours
devoting one second to each Hiroshima.

9.

The real estate agents are lost on Old Dump Road.
Coyote yelps. The last hunter shoots.

The kids break through the woods
still looking for the party.
I throw open the window. *Here's your bed!*
We've kept it warm for you!
You always pull me back to weep in your arms, where

are my teenagers?

10.

The volcano erupted. The world turned to ash.
Now the planets line up: six hundred days and nights.
The sun comes north
falls into the mouth of the Strait.
Rhododendron. Honeysuckle. Calypso. Trillium.
The stunted shrub blazes up
like a flaming heart.

And snow circle of mountains! Ring of fire!
Rainier, Mt. Baker, Glacier Peak, Mt. St. Helens!
Olympic home of the Gods: Sappho, Makah, Joyce, Quinault.
Shi Shi, La Push, Ozette, Kalaloch.
How many nights, my love, how many poems, my great poet
we have awakened

to a low moan of a fishing boat,
someone's voice, almost
heard in the trees

      It has already left. It is on its way.
      It is coming around from the other side of the continent.
      The date is a secret.

      It will enter the mouth of the Strait
      then slip down the Hood Canal.
      It will move beneath your cabin.
      It will come through your windows.

      You will be anywhere in the world
      and it will find you.

—For Michael Daley

from

*SOUTH AMERICA
MI HIJA
1992*

I have a small
daughter, called
Cleis, who is

like a golden
flower

      I wouldn't
take all Croesus'
kingdom with love
thrown in, for her

—SAPPHO

let me, as from conception
achieve gnosis, direct contact
with the depth of all Being

let me enter breath
white jade of perfect lake
until all is refracted
is

Daughter

Divine of my Body

Amerrique

—PRAYER IN LIMA

*Yo hatch katchkani
Manan yo hatch katchkani
Chaimita tapukui*

Out the window, Colombia, out the window
the road beneath the window, the mountain village.
Out the window men on white donkeys, women in a crooked door.
Inside the window, back of the bus
I carry our daughter down the Cordilleras, the Andes.
Out the window armed farmers
carry marijuana to market.

Out the window Bogotá, city of thieves.
Out the window, the guns, the revolutionaries,
the lust of the police. Inside the window
the civil war, *you must take turns,* it is whispered,
to sleep. Everyone has had someone
killed.

Out the window the bus descends the continent.
Inside the bus the driver pilots an airplane.
We fly faster than last night's news warning of travel, we fly
over deep green valleys, mist-filled.
He sees around blind curves, he takes us over
flowering rock walls, landslides, a five-year-old boy
building an adobe house.
We fly past women washing clothes on a rock, we fly
above the clouds, above the road, how many days and nights
washed-out to Quito, around and around
the Cordillera Centro, how many nights
over the fog, over the coffee plants, over the jungle, over the swollen
    rivers,
the cows and clouds streaming down the mountain side, the dark sky
of the East, over the grass huts perched on the abyss, over
these people who never traverse
to the outside. *If we go slow,*
it is explained,
the bandits will stop us.

from III. The Road to Lima

1. PAN AMERICAN

a. They Drive with Their Horns

The earth spins
at its middle the Valley of Volcanoes,
spins the balanced faces of the Otavalos.
Inside my daughter giggles, lots of young men.
The moon rising in the Fish
plucks from inside my heart a music, washes
with its cosmic light the incredible Equador
thousands and thousands
in white knee pants, blue ponchos, Panama hats
streaming down the lunar land, twelve thousand feet the Andes
the local bus descending
to Peru.

The driver and I are the only ones awake.
Descending and descending all night the freezing rain,
the switchback road, the squeals of our tires, the groan
and clutch of the brakes, the snap and scream inside my ears,
the howl of wind through the mountains that loom
as evil gods who watch us,
her head on my shoulder.
On a high precipice hours past midnight el buso
suddenly stops.

Inside a cave a giant white Virgin blazes
inside two dozen wind-whipped candles.
A half-dozen men circle her,
truck drivers, brown-striped ponchos
rising and falling about their bodies
in the wind like pyramids.

Our driver descends to the roar of their greetings,
stoops, puts money in her slot, lights a candle,

blaze of light! bows, then kneels, prays,
his lips moving to the white cement.

Now he huddles with them against the Andean cold
into her flame, lights his smoke, laughs
against the abyss far side of the road.
The black moons beneath their eyes
are ghouls over her shine, over the whipped play
of their sinister robes.

Inside the bus I watch, voyeur.
Will I ever understand el hombre?
the masculinity of worship, the pomp of ritual,
the show of arms, the hoard of gold,
the civic idolatry here in wildest nature,
the machismo of their camaraderie,
the kneeling in each's presence to a stone called Mother
the sex in that

the male spirit of these mountains, volcanoes
spitting ash, this hard
continent, hard driving, my seat broken over the wheel,
my legs aching over our things, my ass, this
rough passage, these tough
passengers, their pungent
smells, oil
of unbathed human leather, spray
of exhaust from holes in the floor, our money
in the slot of a virgin. My baby's long legs
out the window all the night the bus plunges
the Andes to the sea, to the crying
of an ancient violin

      vaya con dios mi hijo
      vaya con dios mi hija

c. Love Song to Strong Wind, Amerrique

If I could write the love poem
of my continent to yours
If I could write my love
to you, Strong Wind,
                       Amerrique
 dead lips would congregate
throughout the earth and I would tell
of the soul
                   (I would tell

of sex

as when I stand in the sun
and see the globe of earth
whirl through space from west to east
and see the holy tear
of the South from the North
in the landmass dance
the drift
the removal of his rib for her
Panama
the way they cut you
for speed, commerce

If I could write of this hemisphere
how in love our two continents, the form of our souls
yin and yang, river of mississippi, river of amazon
how her loins articulate the form of all creatures
how we fit
from each other

the way you swing so far to the west, then tighten
your long phallus
in the uterine ecstasy of the chaotic seas
to reach my fat centers,
my high Aconcaqua, my magic Denali

I would blow, Popol Vuh
El Niño
from Peru to the Bering Sea
the Aleutians' little string
across your Emperor Seamounts
to Russia, Siberia
crumple your islands in the great Gulf
around your sun, bleach
your sands blonde
Caribbean

the way your ocean plates are continually diving down
beneath me

the way Brazil yearns so
for Africa, Aphrodite

     Persephone's vertical descent
     Demeter in her grief wandering horizontally

     this journey backward in time and downward in Earth
     this search for the lost cities, the untraveled,
     this ache for the lost daughters, the unknown
     mothers, this quest
     for the self
     this evolution of the human, holy hejira
     beyond gender identity,
     this return of the fathers
     as Sons to the children
     this search for the Holy Grail
     that contains his essence
     this riding down the world

like writing a love poem
my tongue down your body
this semen   Everyone
born from the body of a man

this sinking to the ground
this prostration to her revolution
this touching my face
to her os cervix

untranscendable mold   Everyone
born from the emotional depths
of woman

All night armies of people and your guerrillas
across my face, an epic poem.
I fall in love the month they kill you.
All night I fall through the Andes,
into you in Bolivia. Into Indians, almas mias
you couldn't understand

All night I take the shapes of older stories
Psyche in her transmigrations
a power struggle on that sunken continent
in which I use the people as pawns
three thousand years of bodies and bodies
hysteria in everyone I create
and everyone one I lose so violently.
I take a female body and lose control
become their oracle in my violent trancing
yes, yes! I was murdered.
In all my lives I am assassinated.
When I wake to this bus climbing the Andes
my daughter is in the window
beyond three Indians, writing in her diary.
I call to her
I love you

then fall back with you in Buenos Aires, Guatemala,
the secret Bolivian valley where we train.
All night I wake and call to her
I love you   I love you

and dream the words *I love you* streaming with light
through the holes in your clothes,
see in a vision the epic structure:
the beautiful globe of blood-streaked earth
whirling through space from left to right.

. . . .

All night through the Andes I bargain with you
clothed now in the glory of their violence,
my daughter, my love poem to the continent.
All night I so love the world, riding the tossed coin down
this foreign road
I display myself

my unforgivable crime of love, your oracle
your eternal punishment of me, my martyrdom

your feet wrapped in filthy rags and pages of my diary
the wings of condors on your back
a rifle in one of your bloody hands

my oracle, your martyrdom

. . . .

from VII. The Heights of Macchu Picchu

2. ALTURAS DE MACCHU PICCHU

c. *I ask you . . . show me . . . allow me . . . to . . . touch el hombre*

Echoes of wind
answer up the narrow canyons.
Thunder rolls through the sheer cut
we came through.
Lightning circles the needle peaks,
Macchu, Waynu.
Clouds float through the streets, engulf
my girl, Shawn Colleen, the jóvenes
who follow her.

Looking far down on a red helicopter.
Quiet. The quiet.
Mantur, the valley, bursts like a shattered mirror
a new world. Silence.

> *The graves found here*
> *are of women*

Yma Sumac, cry and scream! I walk
your streets. Macchu Picchu,
American city of Sappho, Isle of Lesbos,
headwaters of the largest river on earth
down which the Spanish explorer
Orellana floated four thousand miles
to the mouth on the equator
in pursuit of the rumors, the legend
of Amazons

away
from the source, this
nation
of female warriors

I walk through your temples Macchu Picchu
ruin of perfect ruin
aloft with so much death, a wall, with so much life
and pray

    Stone within stone, and woman where was she?
    Air within air, and woman, where was she?
    Time within time, and woman, where was she?

When the furious condor batters my temples
(allow my hand to slide down a hypotenuse
of milk bodice and moon blood!)
I too like the poet
see the ancient being, the slave, the sleeping one
in the fields, I see a body, a thousand bodies, a woman, a thousand
women under the black squall, black with rain and night,
stoned with the leaden weight of statuary:

    Mama Wako, daughter of Viraqocha
    Mama Oqllo, heir of the green star
    Mama Rawa, granddaughter of the turquoise
    Mama, O Mama Mama Mama

        rise up
        to birth with me

        my daughter

from

BODY AND SOUL

2000

. . . and I shall be free to possess truth in one soul
and one body.
—ARTHUR RIMBAUD

Santas

My mother has always had a thing about Santa Clauses. Maybe
a fetish. Come the season she begins pointing them out, that's
a good one, that one's not. By good she means the ones
who are true in spirit, a good that manifests physically
in pink square-round cheeks, large sky blue twinkly eyes, a heart
shape mouth, a nose not too small, not too big and hair
all around the beatific face that waves and sparkles and flows like the sea.
A good one has a real body, no
obvious pillow, not skinny legs. Is large and strong, can hold
at least three children on his mysterious red velvet lap. Is kind, is
Jesus. "Now that's a pretty Santa" is her highest acclaim. I too
have my tastes, I might say biases, a kind of lingering
interest maybe not quite normal. There's my first Santa,
the first one I remember anyway. "That your mother?"
It is from his knee that I can still see my mother standing
outside the circle of presents, beyond the blinking tree. Twenty five.
Looking at him with her scrutiny. My two-year-old brother
has gone first, then my three-year-old sister. I am four,
the age she was when her mother died. I can still feel
the electric current running between his eyes and hers
as they stare at each other as if into the deepest mystery of the Universe.
Maybe the North Pole. She has already begun
my daily lessons in the true meaning of Love.
When my father dies, the Vow accomplished to cleave only unto him,
and that first Christmas comes around without him, she finally
tells me the truth about Santa Claus. The closest she ever came
to having an affair. He would come in where she waitressed,
the Downey Road House, buy Camels from her, play
"Love Walked In" over and over on the jukebox, drink and smoke
the whole pack while watching her serve dinners. She quit,
found a new place in Huntington Park, until late fall when
Love Walked In again. She was so lonely, that was the period
that if they lived now they wouldn't have made it.
She quit there too. And then there he was on that lit throne
in Penny's, the prettiest Santa he ever saw,
her children on his lap. No disguising those eyes, that soul.

What do I want for Christmas? To be as great as she, as perfect
as he. To remember everything. What do I believe? In
the baby born. In Love. In my mother who still believes.

Marrying Ramon at Thirteen

The only time inside his house, small Mexican classic, really
Arab, cream stucco, the archways, the red brick roof tiles
formed over the Indian thighs. Foster home. His tribe
unknown. The den. I always see this. He gently nudges me down
across the tight grosgrain-covered bed.
The room clean, perfect, out of a magazine. Pale
peach cream, sand pastels, sage greens, crimson
bougainvillaea dripping from the tile. Smell
of geranium, swish of pepper, eucalypti release, sway
of palm, the ping ping ping of the red pepper
seeds dropping onto the patio. Pink. Maybe
this is the first time we almost go too far, maybe
the first time the unbearable eros of place, of being
where you're supposed to be, where
you could be caught, the hell in that for both of us, the adults
elsewhere in the house, or gone for a rare moment, the incredible
allure of a bed, of where you're supposed to be
when you make love. "Lura." Sweet sounds, sweet smells, luxuriant
feels, the comfort and cleanliness of the wed. "Ramon." Safe,
not sage not dirt not the dry river bed and rocks not animal shit not human
   come
on the haybarn floor and stucco grade school hall
where we hide to finally move our bodies into each other, the way
it would be if we could marry, this, a married couple's bed, the
Reeves, foster parents like Fosters Freeze, so cold so twisted so man-made
that old man, she so formidable her daybed,
guest bed, his bed I'm hearing now, you
sleep here? Every night? The way love should be ending
in sleep. Warm breeze like a prayer whispered across
their two bodies. The power of it. Of myself of him
of them of all of it. Cacti standing up all around
his handbuilt her handkept house and no signs of the boy. Sentinels.

Under the Steering Wheel

We meet again, you the boy I most respected in high school.
A self-made millionaire, you tell me right off
you've done it morally and your next goal in life
is to become a wise man. You remind me
of what I've never forgotten, that it was you who bought my car
when I married two weeks after graduation, more cherry
than any of the boys'. And you tell me
what I have forgotten, our date to the Junior Prom.

"You said you couldn't kiss. Doubi was overseas
but we could just go together. Then back up at your house
end of the night you said one kiss would be okay.
I got out, you lay back under the steering wheel, your head
on the seat." You tell me this almost as a question, as if
all these years you're still trying to understand
something inexplicable. "Outside I bent over, kissed
your lips upside down like that."

At first I don't remember, can't imagine. But I take your word
for it, strange and out of character. Out of story.
That the question in your aura isn't years
of your one wife's jealousy, her obsessing on your sexual fantasies,
or the locker room gossip still carrying on here. Or of even
a secret erotic image you've never uttered and this is why
you are whispering. (Though if so I am honored.)
I take your word for it, this beautiful picture you give me
though something worries me too, how the slander against me
has never abated since those days, all of my societies
like high school in that ugly way. If I could tell you
the lies told of me. If I could tell you how many times
my heart's been broken, karmically forever
by this hill of persecution I fled, wisdom
would be yours as infinite as the stars.

Then the smell of car plastic, then the feel of my two large
alabaster breasts falling forward to my face

from the coral strapless that had been my cousin Billie Jean's
before she died in the car accident, her taffeta
petticoats and hoop up to the windows. (Maybe
lying back on the seat was the only way to maneuver to your lips.)
Then the perfect round of the steering wheel, then the long shaft
of the column and the pungent sage of Olive Hill
looking up the underside of the saguaro cactus and date palm
and the zillion stars whirling overhead, where we've come from
since the beginning of time and where we're going into extra
galactic space, it comes back clear as the Milky Way, Puchipa
the real ones of this place call it.

So let me explain. How will you begin your study
if you don't know this? I lay down
an odd girl so wise she was already an old man. I lay down
on that seat under that most beloved wheel of my life,
what would become, though we didn't dream it then, our mutual
steering wheel out of there. The smell of plastic
rose to my nostrils, it was
the only thing to do. One kiss
not of lust. Not a broken vow, not betrayal, not
infidelity. Not seduction, not submission (except
to the Cosmos). Not duty, not for material gain. Not
reputation, not abandon, not mindless, not crazy, not
immoral. But

for my lips to meet your lips, for my body
to breathe in your breath. For your body
to breathe in my breath. This was important.
I never dreamed then my life of words from these.
Nor yours of moral money. We were both
so poor then but even then
it was that nothing else
was wise. You and I.
The absolute demand of the moment, the Truth.
A photo taken by the stars.

—*For Richard Smith*

Bride

Nights in the desert I take off my clothes. How long
I have dreamed of doing this. Not having eaten
for over a week—a few boiled eggs, ninety calories apiece,
four ounces of orange juice, forty-five. Something
when I am naked he doesn't like. Humble as I am
I have always seen my body as beautiful, at least as beautiful
as any *Playboy* photograph. Eighteen, I've waited years
to show him. My mother said daily from the bathtub when I was in
    sixth grade,
this is the greatest gift a wife can give her husband. My
virginity. He's in the bathroom brushing his teeth.
The trailer reeks of aftershave. 4:30 a.m.
he'll report to work to beat the sun. I'll pick him up
at the end of the workday, 10:30 a.m., our secret weapon
shimmering on the horizon like a mirage, the burnt men
coming from it. I lounge on the bed writing
my maid of honor a postcard, "China Lake." Being nonchalant,
just being natural, not trying to seduce him. Anything
for him to respond. Is this what I'm guilty of? Pretending
everything's fine? Frying the eggs without butter or oil, I
don't even know that. But I am beautiful. Blue
the veins in the two cubed triangles of marble. In the showers
I saw I was color and shape more like *Playboy* than the others.
But every day since I've been here they have come through
who they were, the visual miracle. Bodies exactly their genius.
Fourteen to eighteen. The marbled fat, the spider veins, surprising
bulges and hollows, purple birth marks, the fear-full
pimpled faces, pimpled butts, shame in the malnourished postures
under the nozzles, the ones—I knew this only
after you were born—who had already had a baby, or at least
started to. I love and miss them unto sickness. My mother
in the bathtub looked different too, not like the ones
on my father's porno poker cards. She never apologized.
I know you hate me for daring to speak of this, all Greece
hated Helen though she was also God's child. I looked

airbrushed. Every bit as technical as the Sidewinder
shimmering over us in the hundred and twenty-six degrees.
I am only trying to find here what was disappearing
when your twenty-two-year-old father found my physical being
beneath him so displeasing. And you exploding out.

Son

The bullet shot through me
and lodged beneath my heart
and swelled and grew until the birth
was a man I rode between my legs
into the bloodstained hands of the world

≈

Earth got inside me
too large you came against
my young girl's will
you came too large, I broke
you were not
you were the first thing not
my will

You were so large in me
the child I was could not know
what was coming

≈

But it was you coming
so large, my child
's body cried and bled to contain you

so hard you were, so hard I tried, I stretched
and pushed and cried
to keep up, you dwarfed me
you were coming, too large

I bled you, I was torn apart in you
my skin you split and shed and left

my belly	too large
broke	I broke
my body	I broke open too large

you came against my young girl's body

～

It was you
coming, my son so bright
it was the golden garden of your hair
I first saw, so large, the light

so large I opened, too large
you were coming. A voice
kept saying
don't be afraid, but

fear is a small thing
death
was born to me when you were born.
The Sunday morning I labored to give you up
they turned the sun back
to wait

Everyone thought
I thought
there were two of you.
You came too large, I
was too young. They laid you
on my ripped belly.
You had outgrown me.

And then you came, too large you came
larger than anything that had ever happened
larger than anything that will ever happen

Shattering everything, Love
ripped through me
the violent encounter of my life
I was not prepared

my heart   broke

open   my

baby   boy

opened

me

I had not known
love before.
I will not know
love again, no man

could ever pull me   like you
turned me
back around
down to you, so small at my breast
too large
        I was not
                prepared
too small
        I was not
                prepared

like the famous Pieta, the too-large
Son in his Mother's lap
we visited when we were

too large with your sister

no one ever
told me, strange
how women never tell

your birth the birth of love for me

your birth the birth of death for me

your birth the death of God for me

God died when you were born
He was too small.

～

I brought you home
the house was too small
the father too small, I

was too small

you lifted my arms
you said grow
you arranged them
around you
you called me
Mother

I loved you

the only thing that has ever matched your size
has been my love for you

～

and you grew little boy I held
and suckled and carried and followed and chased
and washed and dressed and fed and
read to

I was the little tugboat that cried
I was the little tugboat that tried

You kept growing straight up
I kept growing to catch up
I was Jack
I sold my cow for the magic seed
I climbed the giant beanstalk
for the golden egg
I met there

the Giant

my body curled around your sobs
my body in the dark curled around your sleep

my face breaking open
like yours, grew
until our face
became a ball we threw

my son, so tall
my son, so bright, it was you coming
so large, the golden rays
of your hair, in every direction
the golden garden of the world

When I conceived you, I conceived the world
Death was born to me.
Never again did I believe in war
the world too large
my country too small.

So now as you grow
to the age of the soldier
I am unbelieving
that any mother
has ever given
her son
to war

your body so light
grew   I grew
my body grown, grew

and I broke

open

to where you are always birthing

to where you are always leaving

  this too-small girl
  who birthed a giant
  this too-small girl who raised a giant

is pulled and bled and ripped and grown
into the larger world and comes now

large into the world I follow you out

you said grow

you lifted my arms, my son
no longer my son, the son
I love you, you leave me
now I will always be pregnant with the world
you arrange my arms around it

Arrested Love

I remember the tiny room in the worn hills of El Sereno
Los Angeles' oldest neighborhood, the catalpa
tree in red bloom outside. I can't remember
the first time we made love. Was I inadequate? I wasn't
a poet yet. Just that
worry, my young mother's body, you
though a year older still a boy, a
student. (How students are supposed to be
because, actually, I was one too.) I remember
you looking at me from your bed when I came in
off Catalpa, I didn't know Catalpa
is Creek for *head with wings*. But I saw
the first allowing of a glint in your always-blazing blue eyes
that I might join you. There is a memory
of me paralyzed against the wall in my black angora
full-length coat, nothing underneath.
A memory of the crumbling cement steps in the steep
weedy lot next door, my astonishment
that this city has history. Almost
voices in the old Spanish whispering
at the window. Soboba. Chumash. The weeks after that
when they arrested you, the possibility
it would be years, even
life. Being glad we hadn't made love, I knew even then, maybe
especially then, my first marriage to the Russian, my capacity
for fidelity. I remember when like a miracle
you were suddenly released and penniless
hitched thirty miles across that night freeway basin. You
were tight. At the door I saw a cross
between your brows. You rolled a joint, passed it
to me, my first, my love so great
I overcame that impossibility too, all my inadequacies. We made
love on the narrow green couch of my first marriage, my babies
asleep upstairs. Maybe that was the first time. Yes. Pictures
of them beating you when my fingers felt the welts down your back
and me crying and coming. That anyone could hurt you. Two

hearts, whole genitals, whole bodies winging as one. Always
no matter what my body beat with yours as one. My eyes
closed, seeing them again with you behind the bars, Jesus
they're crucifying. The man who loves me
as much as I love him who's always stood
over my bed. My whole self
prayed into you *come back*, my vulva
held you like a mother, your bitterness and blue
coldness. Did you not feel me as your Savior too?
In the morning I wrote in my journal
about your being Jesus, your
long dark curls, your thin anguished Northern Italian face
from your father who disappeared at your conception. Your penis
elongated like Goya's, exactly the great art of our World
and men beating you. I wasn't a poet yet, I didn't know
how wounded you were, how outrageous my seeing
Jesus. My belief that love could heal you. You'd never
be the same boy. No matter, I had seen you
before the Fathers, I loved you enough
for both of us. You and your humor, your marijuana, your
conscientious objections. Me and my kids, my
big Holy Love. We became
Cosmic Pals across the world about to change forever (you
and I were a part of that). But I still wasn't a poet
though I entitled the piece "Are My Bars Not Different?"
I still didn't really know my kind of love, unconditional
feels like prison too.

My Brother's Keeper

There's a moment in my life I want
to make love to my brother. I want
to swim the torrential river between us
and save his life. I want
to put all my body around his drowning body.
I want to pull him into me.

We are in Vermont, our first time alone
as adults. He has come all the way east
across the continent rather than commit
suicide. He's lost his three babies and wife
to his best friend.

Nights he sleeps in his camper
parked on the side lot beneath trees with leaves
like meat turning color. Upstairs
in bed with my love he is out there
like he was when we were kids, on the porches
because it is wrong for a brother
to sleep in the same room as his sisters
and our father when he comes home from the Army
is jealous. To get him here I have raved
about the beautiful college girls of the town.
I didn't understand then
they were mostly Jewish and would not be drawn
to a handsome blond cowboy,
with *Keep on Truckin'* taped in iridescence
above San Diego plates.

Mornings our bodies from the same bodies
face each other in a high northern room
over the Winooski, standing
to sip our coffees and watch it
ice over before our eyes.
He tells me "the big secret,"
the seven years they competed, both making

love to her. "Someday I will win,"
the best friend boasted in the beginning and now
he has, and now my brother's other confusion
about how beautiful she was in his arms.
I am dreaming of reaching across the ice
and pulling my brother to me, to make
the love I have for him actual flesh.
The images float between us so real I know
he must see them too, and so knows
my cowardice, experiences again
love's betrayal. But I am struggling too
to recover from the night with the man I love
who in our high moments begs me to tell him
I desire my brother, to go naked through the snow
to my brother's door. Every morning
I hold my breath that my brother emerge
from the igloo that is his bed.

Our father went around the world to war
and our baby brother took his place
in Mama's bed. We won
but Daddy was never the same.
My brother's legs hurt and sometimes he forgot,
sleepwalked sobbing back to her. Daddy's yells
woke us like nightmares, "Sissy!" "Mama's boy!"
Some mornings we woke to our mother on the porch
curled around our brother in the crib.
Now I am like the Nazis
who placed the naked bodies of young Jewesses
on their dying soldiers
in the experiment a woman
might bring them back to life.

In that huge room at a window like Vermeer
the white stuff starts falling
around our two bodies of desert at flood stage,
debris of the miraculous flesh
our parents risked everything to make.
Then I am like Isis combing all the world

to put our mother's son back together
so mutilated by our other brother
this is the origin of evil
at the beginning of the world

and I want to be a poet
to say my brother the River and the distance
between us. I want to die
to say what a brother is, to name
the river and be the love poem
to the soldiers on both sides, our
father

to be for all time a line out
into the Nile of his severed gonad
inside the fish that's swallowed it,
rowing, Mama, past our more practical sister
lying down with carrion on the battlefield

my body grown dark as a Jew's, the guns
at our heads, the chambers of gas
on every shore, the prisoners
who know nothing now but the fuck,
their mothers cribbed into evidence
against them

and lie down on the cold bronze my brother has become
and suck him back

As We Make Love I See Her Nez Perce Face on Main Street Cursing Me

In our love I want to know hate
her hate as precise as the move you make
to me. I want to love you

enough that your love doesn't die
when she spits
as we're introduced

I want to love the hate
birthing from her cells
her lover dead of our love

I want to make love to you
out of her hate, cover us carefully with her curse
not cover up her heart we raped

I want to touch you I want to bring her with us I want
her in you I want you in her I want to make art
of the three of us   I want to fuck you

until her hate is so loved
never again can your love
be false

Our love, Love, that will last
only if we love her hate

Answer

The secret of the world is hidden in the world.
—CLAUDE LÉVI STRAUSS

After they have gone to bed
my father's low whimpers continuous
with my mother's talking to him,
the sound indistinguishable, almost
from the conversation I heard all my girlhood
from the other bedroom, I feel
my way down the dark hallway past them
to the living room
lit by the moon.

"Is it quartered or full, Sharon Lura?"
his last words to me tonight.
It was the slightest sliver
the last time he asked.
Now it silvers the Siuslaw at high tide, the dunes
on the other side like benevolent souls
stretched out with their corpses.
I watch the brisk visible wind
recarve them.

The gulls are still here beneath the window, hundreds
blanketing the beach to the river's northern turn.
For two days they've been landing.
They stand silent, unmoving
except for a slow back and forth
with the tide
as if waiting.
"Look now," my father said, propped up.
"They've all turned
this way."

I do look. The lunar ray,
a vibrating band, weds me
and for the first time I know

my middle name, moonlight
from his mother. A flash,
the sun's corals and golds still held,
the wind turns
a pulse of light and mist
like an immense
sigh of exhalation
and the cells of everything

open
slightly
as if to show me

the secret

too pure, too silver and crystal to read
but something
of message, even
meaning

in my father's agony, this
suffering unto death

Eagle

The buried images of my father rise
with each stroke of your long fingers, each
bite of your mouth the first time I am made love to
after he dies, his miraculous body laid out, unfeathered
eagle of gold with words moving through and out
"I'm going north soon as I get free of the pilings here."
I experience again the death of his body
the first time we make love.
It starts in his feet, moves in spasms north
like birth, days in labor it takes until he leaves
through the top of his head. After,
I collapse to your massive chest, "What does it mean?"
"It means nothing. We are accidents.
But this is why
I am moved
by our attempts
to each other."
You slip on your grandmother's chartreuse ring,
we go out to walk the streets. Across Portland's
"most beautiful bridge" heart-arched to the Willamette
you ask me "Do you hear voices, Poet?" then "Who
were you at sixteen?" The terrible questions
that feed on our individual bodies keep rising
to enter the other's. As we step onto the shore
Evelyn's stone flashes down there "so old
no jeweler knows what it is"
and now we are standing in a street
of a thinking toward something that cannot
be thought, this degree the sun melts, the gold ladder
of feathers down into the Siuslaw, the dunes
in front of his house where the whales beached when he lived
the whole world their unburied flesh and the blue heron
I long ago named Daddy from your stroke of him
just now from me.

Two Weeks

What do you dream, little boy
oohing, aahing, asking
deep from your sleep
on my breast

I edit an old essay
over your still-foetal form,
having come from the Paris streets,
the archaeological dig under the Louvre,
about the Mysterious I, write
to a poet friend asking why
she casts herself
in the third person.

What do you dream, Little Boy¿
whistling, snorting, hiccupping,
asking. Have you returned
to that place from which you were born,
or are you already in
third person¿

What do you dream, brand new One,
shuddering, sighing, suddenly staring.
Now asking, now telling, now protesting

in a language only my exile
as when I'm out on the streets
keeps me from

War: Old Best Friend

In the dream I reach over to you,
pat your tummy, the place
your son came from, your son
bombing tonight a people
he knows nothing of.
In the dream I am reaching
for your womb, I am telling you
I love you, even in this, Suzi,
even these orders this dream

where our lives do not become
so different.
You lie upon one of my makeshift couches
unladylike, pregnant
in middle age.
In the dream you are going to redeem
your once-holy womb, make again
the perfect child
this time not betray it
this time stop his father
from taking him for puberty
to the whorehouse door

In the dream we are in the old truck again
with the two Indian boys
the day before I marry
bumping down the dirt road
to the Santa Ysabel Reservation.
Only in the dream do I understand
the wrong road taken so long ago
you and I
who had only each other
to share
first blood.

I reach over, pat it okay
the barren place
he's flying from.
I sort of comfort him too
the uniform of masculinity
he's put on
he knows nothing of
hysterical to forget
he came from your womb
that produced
this flying to kill
the foreign men
who dream after dream
bear down on my pelvis
with their exact faces
begging to live

In the dream I pat him safely home
to your womb.
It's the next dream
he knows nothing of
I touch
beautiful mound
that doesn't become a man
to screw his mom
over and over
at the whorehouse door

Susan, I reach over
and contract
in that most painful place
I fall through your skin, Love
the way I used to

kiss goodbye
the dream we had

—*Paris, February 1991*

Twelve Weeks

The last day with you. We dance again. Your head
when I pull you up lays itself upon my shoulder. Like
getting on for the ride, where's
your ticket, Señor? How you fold
into me, how deep your sorrow, how with relief
you accept my condolences, let me
dance you. Oh what grieves you, Monsieur?
Oh why do you sob?

Stanza means room. Italian. I dance you
across the ancient room, your head
propped on the ceiling of Earth's largest room
to the window again. Today
is warm. Your first warm day. Your crying stops. I pray always
to bring you to this window to watch the people
cross down there as they have at this crossroads
for centuries. Rue de Varenne and Rue du Bac. Planned
the most famous assassinations
in the basement. Always I feel you watching
as learning how to be here. That you
are a stranger. That you've come whole, but wholly a stranger.
That you must learn like a prison system the way, the only
permissible way. The way you hang your head
onto my heart as if remembering before the pain
of entering here. The clouds of glory. As if
your flesh, hair, limbs, body and soul of a boy
must grow from all that's ever been
and all that is. War. The assassinated. As if
in that seat when I put you back your loud sigh
is the resigning to the long, longest road ahead.

Now on the metro I fall into every face, torn body, mad mind
out of a woman. Out of a woman, everyone.
The sockless sixty-year-old folded into the stair slab
at this stop. That they all
were you, baby

so new so tender so perfect out of two bodies
out of union. And now out of that world, on the other side
I come upon you again at your mother's breast. Giggling
pulling her nipple, the two of you laughing
in the timeless universal conspiracy nations
must overthrow.

—Paris, France—Lopez Island, Washington, April 10–11, 1991

The War

All night sleeping in my van he in prison. My girl
said that man has my heart. When she saw
where they maced his eyes, injected him
with Valium and now solitary confinement,
no more visits or letters for forty days
she collapsed on the sofa and cried
for two. In this country I dreamed
her on a couch in the foetal position
crying uncontrollably, what she did not do
as a girl. When I woke I hoped
it was me. Not being able to cry
since her son was born into my hands
the night the war started. This has nothing
to do with the war she tells the father
who was not there but who feels the enemy
has come into his house again, taken
everything. This is about him
and me. They see

in black and white, she sighs
though the father's sudden sensitivity caused her collapse too.
He says they will never get free
if he thinks like her. He has to see
his enemy. In the prison
they attack the man who has her heart for three things,
his religion, his mother, and her.
He has something that makes men crazy. She
tries to name it. Purity. Something they want
to destroy. There's no word in any language
to name the relationship the father and I share
in the blood of the boy. At night in the van
foetal. What they are doing
to the man who has her heart. The man
who is father of the boy who loves them both

purely. Let go and the real evil rises. Their
beating the senses out of you. No
language for this family. No nation.

—For Palestine, for Israel

The Poet Laureate of Vietnam

A woman in the trees
changed his mind about the war.
"I'm an unhung murderer. What
saved my mind
was becoming a poet."

He led them into the jungle village.
They killed all the men.
Leaving by sampan he looked up
to where they had allowed
the women and children to flee.
Stony, silent, still sentinels
but for one movement

a tear running down the face
of a young woman
he could have loved.

—For Steve Mason, 1940–2005,
Poet Laureate of the Vietnam Veterans Association

Keintpoos

I wanted to live in Keintpoos' cave of wives.
To lie down with him in his bed. I wanted
to lie down and die

Above me against the sky you called me back.
I didn't want to live when they hanged him.

We wandered east along the border of our two states.
Looking for the Falls of the Klamath, drove through
the Labyrinth of Lava. Hiked down the River of Rocks
to their stronghold, the last stand of the Modoc.

A child stared out from the cave.
Damp, pitch black. It was then
I would have traded all my woman rights, everything
to live those four and a half months
in there with him.

A woman sat on the open ledge when you pointed
west to the Ridge where the Army
gathered and camped. Mt. Shasta
went behind the sky. Further inside
three more. Then suddenly
the cave filled with them. I knew
envy.

The Klamath flows from where the Falls
were dynamited, the land reclaimed.
Where DDT drains the Tule, where salmon.
Where herons, pelicans, grebes, gulls. Where deer. Where Spring
is silent. Where you won't know why
this Hell, where you say you can't.
It's too much pain, too daunting
but dare to ponder why Captain Jack did it. Still see
all sides and claim you love me.

Where can we go now Love but into the collapsed tubes
into the confluence of poisons? Into this ancient eruption.
Into his cave further back where his sons wait.
I study the photo the day before he is hanged. Yes.
I'm in love with him. The day
they are shipped to Oklahoma. I keep
making love with you to make his babies. I'd give my life
for you to know how bad. This man hanging
from the cave opening over us. This child
hanging. Our child to be hanged.

The Border

Were we on the border? Is this why
I'm unsure of where we were?
I was sick, that breakfast, the last place before the train.
There was a window, a sea. You lying on the floor
looking out, sheer flesh-colored curtain in and out over you.
There was a bridge, guards, and you trying to see beyond
into your father's country. Then wandering the sand below.

All afternoon in and out of consciousness knowing
you down on the beach looking to my window
the curtains softly blowing. Wanting to love me. Wanting
to enter your country at last. I saw
you were afraid. That night
we cut across hand in hand on the outside
of the trestle bridge. Still
they called to us. Hey! You can't
go there! The sea crashing on the rocks below us.
We did. For one moment we touched it.

Marriage

Did I go to you enough? Did I give you chance
enough? Did I shift my own perspective
for you enough without losing my ground? What haunts me
is that moment we met, how I saw you across the room
went straight to you and sat down. You shook your head
no. I laughed, you were the first
I ever chose first. Then you turned back marry me.
You said marry me every day over and over through
every love act. Then I bathed you
my groom in the running pearlwhite tub
starting with your feet in the center
of the honeymoon suite above Lake Tahoe
when for the first time you had second thoughts
before the ceremony.

Face

I take the magnifying glass to our photo
tacked here all this time. Quick
sand under your eyes. I forgot. What
was I looking for anyway? To see
what the shining is behind us, my eyes
closed, my head slightly bowed, you
looking so freely into my face. The chrome
of my mother's car. I thought
we were sitting in the Bayshore.
We are standing in the dark outside her car.
It is night on the beach and my birthday, the ocean
is pounding and roaring and yes, that part's memory.
Now I'm looking. Falling into your face again
beyond the chemicals and image that trap us,
into the womb under your eyes, across
the polar cheekbones. The mystics say

we have another face
the original one. This love
defies even them. I never looked
without seeing what they say only in wisdom
can be seen.

Psyche between Two Palms in San Diego

I make it dark with my curtains, throws,
kaffeyeh. Lie down and

rise up above my body. (Saturday night's
in Old Town with my brother's daughter
where the tons of young congregate.)
I'm up here in the skylight I struggled to open
from Oregon's winter sea rust, then gave up
the small panic for fresh air, was collapsing
into myself when I found myself
back up here, looking down
on my little self

tiny, actually, from this perspective.
(As the three of us walked back to Chelli's Falcon
a guy was so caught in looking at her.
I remember that now
as trauma. I couldn't
get out.) And this morning standing in Long Beach
with Seifert in his front garden, free food
planted "every square inch" of his lot,
front sides and back
for anyone in his neighborhood, which he said
in the most loving irony "is depraved, you know"

between his little house, situated
beneath the screaming 405, which is
a Buddhist temple where at the altar
in the living room with his dead wife's photograph,
Yoshika, "the Mother of Long Beach,"
they come to chant *nam-myo-renge-kyo*,
and the hungry children to his screen door
for cookies and baloney,
and my mother in her van named Val
for the first Valentine's after Daddy's death, his

first birthday afterwards   (Last night
in Seifert's kitchen, the eight cats running in and out

we drank wine like the old poets, Li Po and Li Ch'ing-Chao
and he explained that sutra is the sound
and stupa is the sight
of the Structure)   I was seeing
that my mother's cousin
who navigated the Mekong River during the wars
looks like an old Cherokee chief,
and then, actually, so does my mother
fixing our breakfast in Val's windows
so I guess I must be seeing
Christopher Columbus Simmons, their
grandfather

when suddenly I was a girl
stranded between the little plugs of dichondra in Hollydale
I had to weed so they would grow together as solid lawn
which shouldn't surprise me
since I was conceived ten miles west on Redondo Beach
I was born three miles east in Seaside Hospital
and Hollydale is only five or so north.
The strangest clouds were gathering the lead light
around the delicately multiplying particles
that suffocated the child's body I so suffered: what
to do with the self?

and I, up here now, see the body
of a woman hugging the edge of fifty
who still doesn't know the crone
in her search for that girl
but knows before she goes into the night
she will bring it to the mystery beat and blossoming
of its perfect rhythm and sound
the Earth and the cats breathing in and out

and that's when, the body
curling around the self
(my legs curling up around
my stomach and breasts

I see your body, foetal, finite
curled on some couch, carpet, bed,
you
so absolutely contained
(remember when I fell in love with your body
lying diagonally across mine
that night on the beach?
and I
so loving this beholding
I could pick up the whole bundle,
I could sweep my arms around
and pick you up. And then somehow

I do

The Geography of My Soul, 2

There's a curve on Highway 1
north of Cleone where once
I made love with a woman. Sy
Baldwin, poet, whose face
was my mother's so long ago
gone

There are places on the planet
where once you did something so extraordinary everything
was altered. The very ground, intersection
of air and earth, longitude and latitude, manzanita
and dune, owl, ocean, redwood and asphalt altered.
When you drive by years later you see
the act still going on in them. Rhododendron
en perpetua

Deer

deer: OE dēor, wild animal: to stir up, blow, breathe; related to animal, anima, soul

I've been afraid of hitting a deer
so many this time of year
down from the ridges searching for food, water
Love. I hate
that hunting season is mating season.
So all month I've been telling a love story
on myself and a couple I love
who are coming undone, how years ago the three of us
as new poets and they as new lovers
were returning from a reading on the Russian River
a midnight climbing Highway One I'm climbing now at noon
to her new cabin having just received the news
of your death. "He swerved to miss it
and the fawn turned back." Coming around
this steepest, most twisted curve
the buck was just standing there
pushed up against the high bluff, his eyes
flashing red in the lights and, slow motion, I had time
to say aloud oh honey don't do it.
But not enough time to brake or space to swerve
because he did do it, just stepped right out
in front of us, his rack out to the moon and starset
over the Pacific. "Do you know
deer come down the canyon into your yard
at sunrise?" you wrote me once of a night or dawn
you spent in the field opposite my mother's house
"just watching it."

The buck was dead and so was my station wagon.
We pushed them over to the narrow strip
on the ocean side, that road is narrow;
to swerve might make more dead. I made the bed
in the back for the lovers with the maroon and gold quilt
the old Mendocino man gave my husband just before we came undone

patched by his sister from their childhood dresses and pants.
And with clarity, leaving no room for protesting chivalry
I lay down in my bag with the buck bleeding hundreds of feet
straight down to the crashing sea. You
were a man

I could have married
but that you were married.
Love that is poetry ignited between us so holy
infidelity was not a possibility. I made
the bed in the back of my car for the couple,
you and your wife and the family you kept making
and have carried you all this way through the dark
to this fawn so in love too she's
turning back into you.

—For G., for the Baker-Roberdeaus,
for William Stafford, October 1993

Whales

My father spoke of them on the day he died.
Of walking dwarfed amongst them, dead and dying, their giant
greyblack hulks snorting, letting go
on the beach in front of his house.

My little sister was in love with the biologist,
the leading specialist, when he died in a car accident
leaving her house on his birthday. His posthumous book
is with the poets on my shelves though I'm sure much
has been learned since. For years I had the photograph
she took in the boat with him in Bahia de Concepcion

over my desk of three grays mating. One male
from underneath holds the female up, the other
flies through the air, his loopy long thing
aiming for her. No one knew then why. Bisexuality,
perversity, the laws of gravity, Love. This goes on all day
because mostly he misses.

Today my son in from surfing a dangerous Mendocino fall
tells me they're out there, yeah, this early, no one knows
why, El Niño, or what, but they were filmed
on the Farallons, this Orca, this Killer Whale
mother and her baby, this Great White Shark coming for them.
They never knew this before, the fight goes on for fifty minutes,
no one dreamed the whale would win. And then
she was showing her baby how to go for the liver.
She definitely wanted the liver. Whales are definitely
buried inside me
in the Commune of my Soul.

—For Danny

How to Make Love to a Man

Run your tongue down the two tendons both sides
of his neck. Run your tongue back and forth
along the ridge of the underside.
Run your tongue along the ridges of the head, inside his
fingers, thighs, Adam's apple, Achilles' tendon. Wet
the rigid shaft of his calf, the long hairs sticking up from his toes
and the ones lying down over them like little blankets. Love
his ridges, his frigid Soul. Think
glacially. Constant motion, advancing slowly. Remember
penis envy is what men have of each other. Remember no man
can will an erection. Have him enter you awhile,
the knee-chest position to dissolve the ridges. Remember
he's terrified. Remember it's all he wants. Remember
he seeks confidence you know how to handle
his body, you'll grip him firmly enough. Remember for a man
the importance of technique. Remember like gripping
a tennis racket. Remember he's
emotional. When he comes be careful
not to tighten your grip. Be careful not to forget
the battlefields he comes to you from. Forget them, the lies
he must overcome to come to you. Forget
that to be a "man" is to be unjust. Remember his mother
removed him from their bed, deposited him
on the narrow mattress with bars in the cold cell alone. Make
love to all his ex-loves who live in him as surely as he
makes love to yours though he seeks to banish them.
Though he will say so kindly I wish you were free. He
wishes to be free. Help him with trance, wear
silk, light candles, wear levis and flannel, wear
nothing, don't undress. Remember
just dissolve. Remember no jerky movements. Remember
his greatest fear, he won't be able to please you, he'll lose
it, let you down. Remember your walls
to clasp and unclasp him. (Some will resent this, you will know
who. Remember every man is different
and when it becomes the dance

with each's spirit, when the river is more swift
than flesh, when you break through to the place remember
expose yourself. Let him see you. When he comes be
careful not to change. Remember the ridges
that you roamed to get here, the fall
either side. Where the road began. Where you are going.
When he begins to ascend toward the body cavity
forming a firm rounded mass when the ocean synchronistically
booms approval his edge of aggression, when you ride
his aggression till you disremember everything remember
this is time this is earth this is life this is you. Remember
so great is his love he wants all women.

Cojo at the Millennium

His face in the moment I'm stopped in the aisle
looking down on him, his face under the hat,
first seat beyond First Class, plays like the light
on Lake Atitlan, whimsical, always changing.
From under the khaki brim his eyes meet mine. And again.
A voice saying Love yourself as if you're being fed to God.
Once a hero, Army torturer or guerrilla,
no matter. Half his body left
as carrion on a battlefield. But his stature, without
legs, just the trunk
of him is so great I almost collapse to my knees, cry
in his lap, marry
me. A man who's seen enough
maybe you're big enough to love me.

In my seat way back his face as we lift into the Guatemalan weave
of sky floats before me. The right hand
holding the burntoff stump of the left, hurting. He wants
to live, that's why each breath is whimsical, almost a joke. Face
I realize only now lightly burned, veiled
like those thieves and killers in the movies
who wear women's nylons as masks, stretching
the already stretched Indian face just enough
to make him strangely more beautiful. Mystical.
Like the too-taut facelift of a Hollywood star.

At Customs, out of the corner of my eye, I see
a dwarf. Powerful trunk, half-length legs. A gringa
smiling a smile I pray is never on my face. How
do you meet the Other? Again, he looks at me. And again
explosion and fire, then water over my head like baptism.
The face at the mother's breast. I approach
the man with his stamp, his questions. My love
navigates down the ramp
two full duffel bags, one on each shoulder. Mechanical
legs propelling him, first one then the other. I

don't know what to do. Run forward and cry, you
are man enough to love me. Stopped
by the guards, the border. With gallant
he saunters through the door.

It's true I've been sick, brought again violently
to the body. I curled in that dark foreign bed
in Antiqua so foetal I breathed on my own self.
Like prayer to my own heart, own sex, O Love
am I really going to die without meeting you? Loneliness
is breaking me. O Love. Soldier.
Guerrilla. Torture victim, your
commanders overthrown, armies disbanded, you
could meet me now. I could trust enough
to cry in your arms. I could be your legs.
Face of the enlightened one who has nothing to lose
but life itself, you could love me too.

Color of Love

Whatever was lit up in love remains an image
never to be lost.
—RAINER MARIA RILKE

Let me be in the fires of love again, my
mask and your mask burning off
our bodies the way the sun burns
the planet into life. Those times
when you are in me so alchemically
it is less of relationship than an event
of souls. That one night in our years of nights
you are sitting on top of me
coming back again and again like the moon
in all its phases. An afternoon in December
in a tiny room in L.A., our brief reunion, I in my great loss
am on top, your long thin indifferent blue
my thighs gather up into matter, all of you
on the old unvarnished oak beneath,
my long white sleek back only the ceiling, the wood and plaster
remnant spirits and your bony Christ-hands see
moving deeper and deeper into the lost rivers
and channels, the tidal heart setting off floods
and quakes in sync with the galaxy moving into the alignments
that make solstices and equinoxes, December sunsets. Yes
the exact feeling of a particular color I'm living my life
trying to capture in words. Magenta, scarlet, crimson,
fuchsia? Burgundy and pomegranate are too dark. Vermillion too
yellow. Though there is gold. Hot pink. Iridescence. Fuchsia
yes, with electricity added. What is the color
of electricity? Sea anemone. Maybe
in this miraculous moment I regularly re-create like the fluorescent green
and orange eclipsed full moon the night before earthquakes
I'm feeling the color of the blood before oxidation. Blood
without its iron tint, rust, the mud in it that I, lover of Earth
escape in this moment to the pure sweet streak of heliotrope sun
dropping behind the oceanline with my breath
leaving me as a solitary heart beating over the frozen

blue rivers that trace the ruins of yours. Taking solace
afterwards in the dusky peace of Gaea
creating Earth this way, in absolute and complete selflove. In Garnet
deep transparent red, my mother the orphan
curling herself into the most feminine foetal position to die,
the long fleshpink fingers of her right hand
so transparent I saw the ivory inside
curled delicately to her mouth, posture
of purest love, mothering herself, what no one else
had ever done. So finally
so much did she know of love
she did it herself.

The Millennium: Free Him

My real name or Dakota name is Tate
Wicuwa, Wind That Chases the Sun.
—LEONARD PELTIER

I bring into your cell Crazy Horse's white Appaloosa.
He lowers his head to get in, he allows himself to be brought in, his
electric body to be held at the mouth. His back
flickers like a bad connection, like coming to flames
but his four hooves tap dance the cement. He allows me
to unbraid his mane, to brush out with my fingers his beads
to lay in the hollow between your nipples.
There is so much terror I may not breathe again.
He is Eros who cannot be ridden to some clear light
but must be mounted here in this pit. Only here.
His smell fills it. Their eyes
watch us. Every one of your heartbeats
all these years against the cage
waits

We sow the seed of the native tall prairie grass
into the steel. Our tears are enough water.
Your hand reaches for my right breast, the other pulls me down
under the horse where we are unseen by the monitor.
I pull back, wash with my tears your heavy feet
and the dark wave of hair across your forehead when you are young
and the wave back from your large forehead now like my father's.
The grass stems elongate over us. The crickets scrape
their legs together, scrape together the majesty, my body
down on yours like the sun setting over the world, the wind
chasing me. Our bodies

over each other like the skins of the Indians
the pioneers bound their Bibles with
the living flesh
still in their prison museums.

NEW POEMS
2000–2008

This morning I woke into the Body

Hip Hop Hopi Hope

—For the Hip-Hop Generation

The Hopi believe
the Revolution will happen
when there are many homeless people on the roads.
The Beats believed this too, Snyder and Kerouac in *The Dharma Bums.*
These people will be known
by a name that sounds like Hopi.

Hobo
is from *ho! beau!* French
for *hey boy!* a nineteenth-century call of greeting among American vagrants
and American women from the back porches of their farmhouses calling
to the hoe and rucksacked men tramping by
on the roads and tracks
to hire them

a French boy through the haremed girls
to the hungry American boys beating the roads
Beau. Boy. Bum. Bohemian. Beatnik from the Beatitudes meaning
happy, hopeful, blessed
are the poor in spirit, blessed are the meek
and the hip-full mothers

Gypsy is from Egypt
which is really Greek and pronounced
hee hip. Hee hip son. He and her and their son. Ho! Hippie

is a Sioux word
meaning *"he is there, she is here, they are everywhere"*

holy, happy, homo, hepcat, hipster, hippie, homey, helpless, homeless, ho
hippity hop, hopilong bebop and hop scotch to

I and I
from Babylon
to Hip Hop

O Hopi
let us hope

—1976, 1993, 2005

Hitchhiking with Walt Whitman

> I stop somewhere waiting for you . . .
> —WALT WHITMAN, "SONG OF MYSELF"

Mi hija and I are hitching up from South America.
Sometimes it's Little River, across from the market where I birthed
as a poet. This

is a dream I forget. Sometimes my daughter is the man I love
and it is for him we are stuck. But there's an old man
enormous in stature, personality, hitching up ahead of us, leading
the way, his white mane drifting about his head like a storm off the
   Pacific.
Grumbling we're too slow, he hurries across that curve
and white line of highway where it descends to Van Damme Beach,
his beard now blowing around his cane. But

he slips and falls. Miraculously he's not hit
but lands on his head, is knocked unconscious.

I'm certain he's dead, rush down, bend
to his body, touch
his face. The face is a replica of himself
he's made of podsol clay
and left here. I bend over another
I'm sure is him. But it too, though pleasing,
is just another artist's version of his face.

His replicas are everywhere. The traffic stops, the crowd gathers
around the faces, sculptures of flesh and old expressions
displayed on the road, up the bluff, to the whole sky and ocean. I touch
them all, such complicated, beautiful dead faces
when at last I touch flesh,
and he awakens and again leads the way

up the coastal strip, up narrow steps
we've never taken before. Up

the link of Hemispheres, across the Pygmy
stretched to make the bridge. Did you know

that the Mendocino Fault Line
begins in Chile? That's what we learned there.
Like the ancients, we must come up it
and keep going up it. This is a dream
I forget, sometimes even the journey.

—Dream, June 3, 1980. Poem, September 24, 2006.

Before the Fire

"What am I going to do, Mama? You've been my
husband."
"Yes. And you've been my wife."
—AUGUST 14, 1998

I'm bent over her
before the oven door
of the Lower Umpqua Crematory

the first time since infancy
    I am without veils
    to her

    She without the mask
    nursing me

I am talking to her   I am not stopping

    my mouth all over
      the flesh of her face, big Lumbee
        Cherokee cheekbones we first came to
        in America, her sand dunes we hated

      the body

I am telling her
    it's okay it won't hurt
I am telling her
    how great she is how
    beautiful

    I am smoothing her skin (I was always afraid to touch
    the most beautiful face, her
eyes

are the bluest skyblue again
and her smile is of
ecstasy   the wisest bliss   her fingers

curl before her mouth
delicately

       (did he smooth her face
       in the moments I let her go?
       the agony on her face
       when we carried her out, lightest
       birdbone
       into the bright sun

       Or has she become
       the ecstasy of death
       she so believed
       and wanted us
       to believe in?

       now most heavy
       dead weight doll
       I'm murmuring to

the lover on the pillow beside me

murmuring in her ear like I'm waking
to the hungry baby finally   now forever outside me

       (I followed in her Buick behind the mortician's van
       the fifty miles north up the coast, she wrapped in her yellow rose sheet
       and his maroon rug on the floor in the back, my father's ashes
       in the walnut urn beside me. Up through
       midsummer Oregon Coast traffic. (All
       my life I've longed to see through walls
       but I never dreamed you were in that passing truck.)
       "Like the old tradition of the procession," he delighted
       though only our two vehicles.

"Your father wanted to be cremated," she said again last week.
"I never wanted that
until he did. For our ashes
to be put together and spread over the hills of Ramona.
Finally I wanted
what he wanted."

I see the red bricks "just like a barbecue oven," he warned.
I see the bricklayers stacking them, the temperatures set.
He's given me the instructions, has left us alone.
"Take your time." All
is in waiting for me to slide her into his "Cosmic Blue"
      All
engraved in the tile wreath above the door.

My tongue on her face
    could be a poem about learning to talk, she
       taught me to talk   could be a poem about learning to read, she
    a great poem about learning

to write this

is a poem about words
    breath of wind blowing up through the body, cherokee
    wind

    to my mouth on her nipples
    all my first year

about learning to write the love on the pillow beside you
      without reservations
      without infidelity

    like letting the milk down

to the baby   babbling
the milk back to her mouth to write
the trail of tears   out of the caves

(all my life I've longed for this coast line   I still
      cannot write

all this year in the bath with her
to form words with the breathing
out of the cavity of my heart and stomach
"her soft southern drawl"

to her most astonishing
face, Milky
Way star above her eyes skyblue again not the iron
      that was in them
            when she drilled into me again
            that last minute
                  her Third Eye
                  she always warned she had

laid out like a dead bird, all the roadkill we passed
though soul still coming through
the smile of her ecstasy

> *I was born to grieve for you, Mama,*
> *what you couldn't do*
> *I was born to be your greatest lover*
> *to write your story*
>
> *I became your wife*
> *to be the husband faithful to you*

January 1, 2000, 3 a.m., the Caspar Headlands

I wake inside my mother. Just behind
the thin wall of her stomach, behind a thin wall
of her. Exactly her. Flesh
infused of her. There are no words
inside the flesh of my mother
the edgy raw red-rose cellular wall of my mother

heaving herself on a musical note
from the echoey porch
to call me down Roosevelt Avenue, *"time to come home, Sharon Lura
time to come home"*
those sounds, that feel, before words

a rosy soreness in the quarter inch between me and the world
like earth breathing, like earth thinking (better not come
better not yet, Sharon Lura. In the last weeks

I bathed her. Discovered
her famous red head's complexion
was actually darker than mine. (Famous
to herself, to us in her Story.
Redder. A red skin. Redder
than her pink-white hands, my father's blue-white claws, though

that part of her flesh never knew the sun
or air or eyes (except his. Isn't that
extraordinary? We humans.
Mostly unseen. No words
for this but redder

is a word that comes close to the feel of my mother
from inside her (I had forgotten. Flesh
imbued with her, exactly her
Third Eye everywhere in the red rose petals
I washed, aureoles rosier than mine. *Poof!*

she gasped looking down on them, *poof!*
to the wilted roses of Daddy's dead lust.

      Out the window white Orion lies down
      on the black ocean horizon,
      our blue planet self this night, this minute
      turning across Time's invisible line
      she was so determined to make, their first goal
      as a couple in 1938. The same sky
      over the same headland I am making love on
      two decades ago this night. Two thousand years ago
      some two exactly this night.

      The gods don't have flesh and feel. Star-skeleton Orion
      doesn't know this red inside his mother. Whatever else

      we are flesh.
      Blood.
      Ancient Earth
      about to birth.
      Blood moon eclipses
      aureoles

      wholly her

Bombing Baghdad Again

—For Emily, who wanted me to be her stepmother.

I was a little out of my mind, we were bombing Baghdad again.
So you took me to Lake Woahink.
For Emily, you said. I was glad

to look on that beautiful water
your daughter's date drowned in Saturday night.
I was a little out of my mind, our president
bombing Baghdad again.
I could only stare at that water, only ponder
the Senior Party

that he didn't make it across
Woahink and our woes, ponder
his parents bearing this

this single unendurable loss so accidental
this random mass murder of everything
so deliberate, Emily forever now
the mermaid she was for Halloween,
her feet we bound, her face we veiled,
pulling the boy to the surface
just to meet our bombs

Take me to Baghdad, I said,
looking at that water.
I'll marry you if you'll take me to Baghdad.
You who have plied me with everything
said your first no. Emily

if I could bring back your boy, our boys and girls, his boy
to his body and your dad's, I'd marry him like that,
no other strings, for all our woes

but the President
says no

—*June 30, 1993, and again, March 20, 2003*

Terror

A river is flowing around and through
my heart, sometimes
down one breast, then up the other

now above my navel washing
through the ribs, now waterfall
back over the heart. I know
this river, all those times
love hurt me

I keep waking to the flood, O River Adrenalin
she said was the headwaters
of her disease

I keep waking on a side street
behind Mendosa's in Mendocino, now here behind mi hija y nieto.
River named Fear my Seminole great grandfather was born on, then
fled, his life on the run, in hiding, mine too,
that this family be here now, O Cape Fear
coursing through my solar plexus, this back street
in Berkeley.

Is not the heart in the solar plexus the will to live? I wake
in the body of my killer, his egg splat against my side,
our marker in the road
of the other and self, in
forgiveness. O, Invisible River

I wake in each night, then talk
myself to the banks, this is how you swim

back to the world
that rivers you

—*October 2001 (Mendocino-Berkeley)*

Be Ahead of All Parting

I lay on Emily's grave
I lay on Chief Seattle
as though they were behind me
as though now were that night

For among winters one is so endlessly winter
I fled my love in Lourmarin and found
Albert Camus. I brought back to my love the lavender
that covers him and Madame Camus. All things
double on one another especially our hearts. I sat on Sartre
and de Beauvoir, "Ensemble!" the guard shouted,
one on top the other. I was looking for Vallejo
but found in the slot Jean Seberg. (I didn't find
Joan of Arc or Romain Gary.) On Gertrude Stein
among the pebbles and Alice B. Toklas
I left my Wite-Out, there being no pebbles
left in Paris

We walked across London to Karl Marx
miles covered by asphalt and concrete. My Marxist love
had a fit for fear I'd pee on even his cement. Systems
impossible in time, I am forever dead
in the women's section
of the Moravian Cemetery
in Bethlehem, Pennsylvania, Hilda Doolittle
as "Mrs. Richard Aldington"
beneath the towering phallus
or was that the omphalos? the now that is night, glacier

cloud drifting but mostly
the unknown

when I was going I stopped
at every death

Primitive

Every Sunday the women of my family rose
and moved over to the men of my family,
knelt down and untied
the boots. Pulled the socks they'd knitted and darned
from the thick white ankles, from
the calloused corned heels, from the long arches, from
the hairy white toes. Washed and oiled
feet. In the white church
built by the men, on Beech Hill, on Preston Ridge
in Lynchburg, Tennessee
Phoebe and Fannie and Lora Rae and Nancy
pored themselves
unto Love.

I like to think they weren't prostrating themselves
to snakes, but writhing with, rising
the same, speaking to
tongue in tongue. Like to hear
in that singing that singing still
unto feet. That hissing too, Mary
Magdalene. That tongue onto. Like to hear
my great grandpa sigh Jesus, remembering his mother sigh
long before he wrecked himself with The War.
Like to see his most hated boy, my grandpa Avon
still on the women's side
watching his pa allow his ma
to remove his shoes
and out the window
his shoeless brother
of the newly liberated ones
exiled now to the ditches,
suddenly daring to show his dark face
in the holy morning sun,
and his sister too of our fathers' feet

I gratefully now turn my own self upon
onto   unto   into   until   only
our human oil, corns and calluses,
the unknown miles Oedipus walked,
our fish journey through the turbulent wombs, snakes
and tongues, O millions back
from which we expel. Ever onward
soldiers. Thy kingdom come. This
Living Flesh
we dance   we dance

100 Memories I Don't Remember

The dress I was wearing when my brother was born, my bangs
growing out. My father
undressing me under the house
in Ramona, my sister reporting this
again and again, my white
Maidenform bra

I am trying to tell my sister
or someone downstairs
to save the rotting lemon
because it's organic. We can't remember
everything. We can't forget anything

the last hook, then snap of the band
with the half-inch seams
I always had to make
both sides of the 34D
to fit my girl frame

The migraine up Clevenger Canyon,
there's a grainy black and white of this, I'm
16 in a white V-neck Orlon sweater holding up my heavy hair
having pulled over on that dangerous spot. Having
Vicki take the picture because otherwise
I'd never remember that I
had a headache.

Daddy and my brother were boys
but not different from me,
Mama and my sister. I thought of their things
and our things like clothes we put on. Male
and female, this is how I understood adjective.
I believed with the fervor of prayer we were the same. I still believe
we are the same.

Daddy in his bath shows me how he masturbates,
the word more forbidden than witnessing masturbation
and I don't remember through all the years ejaculation.
He lies in the tub, his big-boned, white hairy body
in the bubble suds. His hairy toes turning on the hot water faucet
to reheat, that's how long we've been in here, his hairy fingers
around his purple thing

> *and what is a mistake? and what is remembering? what is*
> *a sin, instinct, desire, what is*
> *allowance of the self, what is*
> *justice and what is love? Running*
>
> *away, disappearing into the fog*
> *to Korea   to Europe ravaged*
> *to the river bottom, my father*
> *ravaged   Going back*

to the house the first time after I told
my mother in her bath, last week of sixth grade. I remember
flying through the house, leaping off the porch
knowing the greatest relief I will ever know, Mama
will take care of it. But imagine
going back and Daddy coming home.
I remember her beautiful body in the bubble suds, I
don't remember going back to the house, I never
thought to try though she was never the same, I was never again
her child, I didn't know this until now. I always thought
my not remembering was good, this is how we forgive, this is love.
I so loved my mother and my father and my sister and my brother.

Last night I nightmared again
the murdered girl. What to do
with her body? I can't remember who she is
but I remember the Los Angeles River still free
though it had flooded before I was born
killing so many it had to be cemented.

I don't remember the Fathers castrating me

stuffing my mangled, bloody genital into my mouth,
their faces can't be looked at.
I don't remember my gender, my father, my tribe, the fear
but I remember my mother is lost
so my heart rises to go to them
fleeing back down their many mansions
then unable to weep, to remember how we walked
the millenniums, each a galaxy of blood
a hundred billion ancestral faces looking up, if
you are found guilty, Daddy, will they execute you?

I remember my first song, "shu shu m' baby."
I remember going into that forbidden place, myself
that island rising up on the horizon.
I forget its name
but I remember when
it saved my life

Memory Is Pictures Inside You

rivering through before language
the way Moonlight whimpered as he watched
the movie in his sleep. Something
is happening, his four legs are following
the story line. One part of the brain works
as a camera, taking pictures, another part
puts it together. Edits. Which part
is the soul? O Tower of Babel, whoever is
the Self? We can't remember
everything, we can't forget anything

I can't remember the first time we made love.
You said you'd tell me everything you knew
about the woman who was having the affair
with my husband, your wife. But I remember your bathtub,
how you would let me escape there
and how then, after soaking, I'd say come in

Homeless on Good Friday

I saw them on Market, I passed them coming down.
It was 3 p.m. but I didn't believe my eyes

Identical twins.
Boys. About 50,
though their identical rag-and-bone, identical banged-up filth
may have made them
look that old.

Tall. Long gold locks from silver burnt plates
to the crosses of their white tee shoulder bones.
Four redrock cheekbones besot of asphalt, crowns
pockmarked long ago, now from sun, cold, exhaust, maybe

40

It was 3 p.m. but I could not believe my eyes
two of them, identically emaciated, coming up Market,
their morning shaves their gleaming accomplishment,
passing Grooves, Elvis singing to his twin
Hey Jess, it's lonely, come home.

Imagine having your homeless bro
in the sack with you on the sidewalk, imagine
that home (your mama's womb

Now I'm sure
they were 33

This is

a good day,
me and my soul

Love in the Ruins

down on our sidewalk
two days and nights now
the 20th anniversary of my father's death

down behind the weekly painted cement wall
of the new Octavia on-ramp, Sunday night

they were so conked out, her face
straight up, flaming red, so exposed I thought dead, he
on his back, his black pant legs like the sawhorses
my father used to make
and again, last night, they hadn't moved
and this morning, the weather changed,
just a big orange and purple pile
between the two loaded shopping carts

but coming back
striding through somebody's notebooks and loose papers
scattered up and down Market,
a strong hand in my feet, *to resent*
is to give away your power, she

was risen up over him young and fresh
(though something weird and dirty
like a rubber belt for padding or maybe blood
at her exposed crack), most tenderly over
his still unmoving form, his sawhorse to the sky, his black
business shoes to the ground, bent to him so intimately, talking,
coaxing him back, her red ponytail blowing
in the first ocean breeze of Fall
as sexy as the one beneath the headline, "High
End Fashion on the Rise in Union Square"

I never saw his face, but today is the 20th anniversary
of my father's death. That day
in the Oregon dunes

he left us his body (that day I'm still bent
to his face

When I was a little girl I wanted to grow up
and be a hobo with my Daddy, singing we ain't
got a barrow of money, we may
look ragged and funny. My first stories
were of the last couple
at the end of the world
after the Bomb
wandering from devastation to devastation
knowing they had to make love

Now past September, so suddenly Daddy
the weather has changed
and they are gone, and you
singing our song

Sally Hemings's Dress

When I put on Sally Hemings's white dress
I found myself stepping up the highest building in Virginia.
I pulled it off and draped it over the steeple's cross.
When the sun rose I was standing there naked, the father
of my children. And when the sun set
I was the moon and all the stars, the father
of my country.

This doesn't mean I don't love
Thomas Jefferson in his pants.
Of course only in Heaven
does he get to wear a dress.
Here even the President can only lie down on the bed,
drape it over himself and sigh
what am I to do with this?

When he puts the cigar in her vagina
the highest building in the land
collapses brick by brick. The Dress
goes up in flames, semen of sunrise, noose
strung from the oak around his neck, bloody cock
in my bloody black mouth.

But O Moon you rise again, Virgin impenetrable
and I step through the sky in my beautiful dress
issuing forth all the Union and Confederate Dead
in theirs.

—Thanks to Charlottesville artist Todd Murphy,
photographer Andrew Shurtleff,
friend Alan Scouten who sent me the news photo,
and to Jack Hirschman's "Blue."

Loving Che Again

I fall in my little bed
my narrow slot on the floor

find my left hand
has found my right

is holding it
tenderly

solemnly

A wing flies out the left side of my heart
from the right side that is hurt

My wing stretches for All
from my little self
        that comes in on the right
            My little heart

comes in on the right
                    rightfully so

But when it caves in
        it flies out
            the left side

righteously

                              —*Berkeley, March 3, 2005*

Abu Ghraib. Guantanamo Bay

You can't unring the bell, he admonished,
meaning 1948, Israel.
So all these bells are ringing, Nazi, Kamikaze
waves out into the universe forever
and I have seen you, as you were never meant
to be seen.

Anyone who peers into the face of God
dies, that was my girlhood religion. Now
I'm made a war criminal. You can't
unring the bell. I am complicit with this front page

So what do I do, O male,
having seen beautiful you?

Apologies, apologies
How dare I say such? But beautiful yes, your faces beaten
but not beyond recognition.

Am I to turn away and say I didn't see you naked and bound together
your tortured, living flesh?
Am I to say tears didn't well for seeing the beautiful boy, beautiful
son, beautiful father, beautiful brother, beautiful husband? Beautiful
lover, am I to say I didn't see
God? I kiss

the torture my words cause, this humiliation
I swallow, this violation your God
will further punish you for, strike me dead on the spot, this
is why this is happening to you, my fault.
I kiss you anyway. I love you. I run my hands down all of you, veil
against our depravity, against our God doing this
to your God, a prayer
that you aren't further pissed on
in the shower. This is not sexual torture
no matter what is said.

I cannot leave you
on the water board, your
broken knees I go down to
sorry

sorry

the electrodes on your genitals, this is not
to arouse you against your manhood
but to drink our bleach and acid water forced down you
now toxic waves forever, my mother's son, my sister's
boy, my children's grandfather, my
lost soulmate, my Ishmael, my Israel, your decapitated
head rolling away, our grandson
packed in ice, nameless
in a secret prison

O Holy   Holy I step through
all our Gods
I know who you are
I know what my country is
I kiss you alive, I do not die
I make you again in my body
I give you my breast, warm sweet milk, I kiss the bruises, the burns, drilled
    holes, cable rapes, castrations, broken femurs, stretched spines,
    crucifixions.
I take the blindfold off

O Holy Face

I recognize

I do not die

O Holy Body

I pray this past our violation of All,
a bell ringing forever too

Prayer

He told me that at the abbey in Kentucky
they just lay the dead in earth. No
box, nothing

      May this be my body's Luck

But so many dead priests they've run out of room.
So now they dig up the old graves
and make a pillow of the bones
for the new head to rest on

      May this be my Love
      come at last

NOTES

from *HARD COUNTRY*

Love Song for a Man Whose Mother Killed Herself

after Adrienne Rich

from Visions of a Daughter of Albion

This is of course an allusion—actually an answer—to William Blake's rather astounding poem (about sexual love, jealousy, and "the soft soul of America"). I was living on Albion Ridge in Albion, California, a part of a writers' group, The Daughters of Albion, when I began this poem, the first of what eventually became *Hard Country*.

" . . . what is this place to me if you are lost?" from "The Islands," H. D.

"My soul can find / no well of clear water," from "For the Union Dead in "Alabama," Ed Dorn

Crazy Horse

Crazy Horse's story, as told in the extraordinary biography by Mari Sandoz, is that of a mystic, a hereditary medicine man who because of the times in which he lived became a warrior and leader of his people. His story is equally a great love story and a story of the psychological effects of genocide. In my poem I am struck by a number of "dream adaptations" from Sandoz's book which I was reading March 25, 1979. The ominous presence of the black marriage robe (a dominant article throughout the book): due to the political circumstances of the Plains tribes at the time, Crazy Horse was unable to marry the woman of his choice, Black Buffalo Woman; he married instead Black Shawl Woman, to whom he was a devoted husband. "I braid grass stems into his light hair": though full-blooded Oglala (for seven generations anyway) Crazy Horse had blond hair; his childhood name was Curly (this was one of the reasons he was called Strange). "I will grieve through seven generations" The oral tradition of the Oglalas, their history and stories and genealogy are brought forth seven generations. "I pull him on the back of my horse": In the last great battles, Crazy Horse was rescued twice by Cheyenne women warriors. "On the Holy Road": The Holy Road was the first white man's road through the North Platte Territory of the Sioux. "I am careful not to hold his arms down": Crazy Horse's warrior vision was that he was invincible, indeed invisible, unless one of his own people held down his arms. Needless to say, when he was stabbed to death in 1876, in a betrayal most likely instigated by No Water, the jealous husband of Black Buffalo Woman, Little Big Man, was holding down his arms.

Appalachian Song

"see a road inside myself / and on it I am running," from "The Edge of "Wisdom," Gerald Malanga

"Call my name in the act of love," from poem of the same title, Michael Larrain

from *PSYCHE DRIVES THE COAST*

Ground Zero

Section 8 from *Lightning East and West*, Jim Douglas

from *SOUTH AMERICA MI HIJA*

Epigraphs:

"I have a small daughter . . . " The Sappho translation is from Mary Barnard.

The third language here is Quechua, the second official language of Peru and Ecuador, the language of the Incas.

Yo hatch katchkani
Manan yo hatch katchkani
Chaimita tapukui

To be
Or not to be
That is the question

from VII. The Heights of Macchu Picchu

The Spanish throughout, and my English translation allusions and uses, are from Pablo Neruda, mainly *Alturas de Macchu Picchu*.

from Epilogue: The Dawn, Amor Amerrique

"The Return of the Goddess": title from *The Return of the Goddess*, Robert Graves

"There Is a New Eve Who Comes," from "Tribute to the Angels," H. D.

from *BODY AND SOUL*

Keintpoos

Keintpoos is the Modoc chief more commonly known as Captain Jack. The Modoc Wars took place in the northeastern corner of California in 1873 along the Oregon-Applegate Trail. In a tragedy-riddled episode involving the demand for a statement of tribal solidarity due to looming genocide, Keintpoos killed General Canby at a peace conference, making Canby the only regular Army general killed in any Indian war. Keintpoos and three of his subchiefs were hanged at Fort Klamath, October 3, 1873, and the Modoc people sent as prisoners to northeastern Oklahoma, where most of them died. The few who survived were eventually returned to the Klamath Agency.

Rachel Carson's *Silent Spring* (1960), generally acknowledged as the initiator of the modern environmentalist movement, tells the twentieth-century story of the Modoc's land, the Tule of California and the Upper Klamath Lake of Oregon: DDT from the surrounding reclamation lands drained into wildlife refuges, killing all life.

Deer

" . . . that road is narrow; to swerve might make more dead," from "Traveling Through the Dark," William Stafford

NEW POEMS

Hitchhiking with Walt Whitman

The ancient pygmy forest of the Mendocino coast grows in the shadow of the redwoods. The soil is podsol, a white clay that stunts all growth. *Podsol* is a Russian word, from the Russians who settled on the coast in the early nineteenth century.

Be Ahead of All Parting

This title from *The Sonnets to Orpheus*, Rainer Maria Rilke

Sally Hemings's Dress

Sally Hemings (1773–1835) was Thomas Jefferson's slave, the half sister of his wife, and the mother of at least one of his children, a fact that Jefferson and Hemings's descendents never lost or forgot, but which has been vehemently, indeed viciously, denied from the beginning by ex–slave owners, white church leaders, politicians, and scholars. When the DNA proof came in, the artist Todd Murphy began a series of art evocations and depictions of Sally Hemings, and in September 2001, when a proposal to name two Charlottesville streets after Sally Hemings or her descendents was pulled from the city council's agenda, he climbed to the top of the old coal tower downtown, in direct line with Monticello Mountain, and mounted atop it a thirty-foot white dress around a metal form. The dress, repeatedly vandalized, ripped and shredded, continued to billow over Charlottesville for several months. Andrew Shurtleff's photograph of the dress appeared in the *Charlottesville Daily Progress*.

ACKNOWLEDGMENTS

Some of the new poems in this collection previously appeared in the following publications:

Big Bridge ("Abu Ghraib, Guantanamo Bay," "Be Ahead of All Parting," "Memory Is Pictures Inside You," "100 Memories I Don't Remember," "Terror"); Five Fingers Review ("Sally Hemings's Dress"); Manzanita Quarterly ("Before the Fire"); New College Review ("Homeless on Good Friday," "Love in the Ruins"); PoetryMagazine.com ("Primitive"); TheTimeGarden.com ("Love in the Ruins," "Primitive," "Sally Hemings's Dress").

"Bombing Baghdad Again," "January 1, 2000, 3 a.m., the Caspar Headlands" appeared as part of the Sore Dove Press Broadside Series (2005).

"Hip Hop Hopi Hope" appeared in Oakland Out Loud Literary Anthology, edited by Karla Brundage and Kim Shuck (2007).

"Sally Hemings's Dress" appeared in Petaluma Poetry Walk: 10-Year Anthology, 1996 to 2005, edited by Geri Digiorno and Bill Vartnaw (2007) and Words Upon the Waters: A Poetic Response to Katrina by Bay Area Writers, edited by Karla Brundage (2006).

The selected poems in this collection previously appeared in the following books by Sharon Doubiago:

Visions of a Daughter of Albion (chapbook) (1980)
Hard Country (1982, repr. 1999)
Psyche Drives the Coast (1990)
South America Mi Hija (1992)
Body and Soul (2000)
Greatest Hits (2004)